Trinity Tales

Trinity College Dublin in the 2000s

This book is dedicated to the memory of Dr Emma Dunphy, who would have had something to say about every essay herewithin, but who would no doubt have refused to write her own. We miss you immensely.

Trinity Tales

Trinity College Dublin in the 2000s

edited by SORCHA POLLAK
and KATIE DICKSON

THE LILLIPUT PRESS
DUBLIN

First published 2021 by
THE LILLIPUT PRESS
62–63 Sitric Road, Arbour Hill
Dublin 7, Ireland
www.lilliputpress.ie

ISBN 9781843518105

1 3 5 7 9 10 8 6 4 2

A CIP record for this title is available
from The British Library.

Set in Minion with Akzidenz Grotesk display titling by iota (iota-books.ie)
Printed by Graphy Cems

CONTENTS

Foreword • Senator Ivana Bacik • **vii**

Introduction • Katie Dickson and Sorcha Pollak • **x**

The Future Was Infinite • Jarlath Gregory • **1**

Rocking the Delicately Balanced Charade • Sallay Matu-Garnett (Loah) • **7**

For the First Time in My Life, I Felt Alive • Katriona O'Sullivan • **13**

Success in Failure • Kieran Quinn • **21**

Slipping Through • Cliona Loughnane • **29**

'And So You Shall' • Annie Colleran • **37**

A Year in a Thousand • Sarah Benson • **44**

On and Off the Stage • Erica Murray • **52**

Playing • Emma Gleeson • **60**

What's in a Name? • Jess Majekodunmi • **62**

Popular Literature • Adam Crothers • **70**

Cobblestone Ambivalence • Caitríona Lally • **73**

Dulyn • Heledd Fychan • **81**

From Russia With Love • Carl Whyte • **88**

'Educate Yourself That You May Be Free' • Paul O'Connell • **95**

One World on Campus • Khalid Ibrahim • 103

Hindsight • Elske Rahill • 109

Shapeshifting • dave ring • 118

Teach Me, I'm Irish • Jonathan Schachter • 123

Changing Trinity, Changing the World: A Personal Reflection • Rory Hearne • 132

Low Buns • Kate Kennedy • 141

The Stanford Marshmallow Experiment • Darragh McCausland • 146

Two Little Boys • Wayne Jordan • 153

Confessions of a Nerd and Other Stories • Claire Hennessy • 159

Adventure of the Unknown • Uché Gabriel Akujobi • 166

In With the Old • Dylan Haskins • 173

Quantum McMuffin: On Learning To Learn • Hal Hodson • 181

Champagne at the Hairdressers • Alice Ryan • 187

FOREWORD

senator ivana bacik

A NEW INSTALMENT of *Trinity Tales* is always welcome. But it's sobering to realize that the contributors to this edition all started their university education around twenty years after my own graduation – they seem very young! It's also sobering to reflect on the immense changes that have taken place over the decades, as revealed within this text. Re-reading the reflections of my own contemporaries in the 1980s *Tales*, what comes across most strongly is our collective sense of gratitude. Because of the bleak political, social and economic context, we felt privileged to have the chance of escaping reality at college, prancing around the cobblestones like characters from *Brideshead Revisited*. In our time, a Cold War divide persisted between the United States and the Soviet Union; apartheid prevailed in South Africa. In Ireland, the Catholic Church remained all-powerful in dictating social policies, and horrific brutalities were being committed in the North. For us, the ongoing grimness of prolonged recession and mass unemployment, and the anticipation of inevitable emigration, provided a stark backdrop to our student lives.

Yet, in spite of all the grey clouds overhead, we had great fun on campus in the 80s; the music was fabulous and the parties legendary. And a distinct sense of social change was already in the air. As Mary McAleese wrote in her foreword to the 1980s volume, the 'last tiny petted cohort of students' were finally being 'rudely supplanted by the arrival on the scene of the more numerous first-generationers ... education-hungry youngsters from humble and modest backgrounds'. This increasing diversity was palpable. The Law student body was enriched by an influx of exotic creatures from Northern Ireland – and while plenty of us were middle-class Dubliners (in my case via Cork and London), many more were genuine first-generationers from beyond the Pale. Trinity was a very enticing prospect then for bright teens from rural Ireland, with its whiff of forbidden liberalism; condoms could even be purchased on campus, and when I and other Students' Union officers were threatened with prison in 1989 for distributing information on abortion, our Law lecturer Mary Robinson heroically took on our legal defence (she kept us out of jail!).

How things have changed since then. The 1990s saw the decriminalization of homosexuality, the legalization of contraception and divorce and the beginnings of the economic boom. Peace broke out in the North, and Mary Robinson was elected President. Internationally, the Soviet Union was no more, apartheid had ended and Clinton was in the White House. Contributions to the 1990s *Trinity Tales* were later critiqued for 'dripping with privileged nostalgia'. But maybe it's understandable to look back on the 90s with nostalgia. In Ireland, it genuinely represented for many a decade of progressive change and economic prosperity.

And so to the Millennium and the experiences of this new generation of Trinity students. Clearly the context for their college years was vastly different to that of ours in the 1980s. In the contributions to this volume, we see fewer references to international movements, the politics of Northern Ireland, or the influence of the Catholic Church. But what is similar, unfortunately, is their awareness of a grim economic context. For them, the heady excesses of the 'Celtic Tiger' were followed swiftly and brutally by the 2008 financial crash, bringing with it the realization that distant 1980s emigration experiences were to be replicated for another cohort of Irish graduates.

More positive common themes do also emerge, however. Like us, those who entered Trinity in the noughties write that they felt trepidation and excitement on first walking under the Front Arch. Like us, they felt anxiety about 'fitting in'. And, like us, over successive years most found intellectual stimulation and formed enduring personal relationships. A further common theme lies in the increased diversity of the student population in this recent decade. What's evident here is the vital work of the Trinity Access Programme in opening up new routes into college for students from traditionally under-represented communities. This text reflects the extent to which more socially, politically and ethnically diverse voices have come to represent Trinity during the noughties, leading to the welcome subversion of the old 'Trinners' stereotype of privilege.

At the time of writing, colleges remain closed due to the global COVID-19 pandemic. In accordance with national public health guidelines, staff and students may only enter the Trinity campus for 'essential' reasons. Academic teaching has moved online; communal facilities are shuttered; library access must be booked in advance. The future is uncertain and, again, grey clouds loom over us all. But one thing is certain: for all current students – and indeed for all recent graduates, just as for my own generation – further massive social and economic change is now underway in Irish society.

Ivana Bacik is a barrister and Reid Professor of Criminal Law, Criminology and Penology at Trinity College Dublin. She was a Senator for Dublin University (first elected in 2007; re-elected in 2011, 2016 and 2020). Her research interests include criminology, feminist legal theory and equality law; her publications include **Legal Cases That Changed Ireland** (co-edited with Mary Rogan, Clarus Press, 2016). She chaired the Oireachtas 'Vótáil 100' Committee programme in 2018 to mark the centenary of women's suffrage in Ireland. Ivana was elected as a Labour TD in the Dublin Bay South by-election in July 2021.

INTRODUCTION

katie dickson and sorcha pollak

IN THE SUMMER OF 2003, I did a brief internship for the Lilliput Press, shortly before starting a year-long sabbatical position as Deputy President of the TCD Students' Union. After graduating from Trinity with a BA in English Literature and Philosophy, my career path took a leisurely stroll through teaching and into librarianship. I therefore hesitated before agreeing to take on this project; I knew that my own professional experience lay far outside the realm of editorial work. I am a school librarian by trade.

I was in Trinity in May 2019 for a dinner for ex-Students' Union officers. We were taken on a tour of House 6. (For those uninitiated, House 6 is the building in Front Square that hosts the Students' Union shop, the SU offices, the Publications Office and many of the society rooms.) We were brought upstairs and I was shocked to find that the SU Bookshop was no more. This had been a space that was central to my own Trinity experience, and now there were only couches and microwaves where once there had been shelves of books.

I started working in the SU Bookshop around Christmas of my First Year. I had applied for a position in the co-op in a spur-of-the-moment whim when I saw an ad outside the SU shop downstairs in House 6. At the time I didn't realize how important this job would be. The SU Bookshop became *my* Trinity experience. And, other than a small, faded sign above the door, there is no longer a trace of it. No longer a *physical* trace, but of course the friendships and the stories live on. I regularly come across books on my shelf with the familiar pencil pricing and code, letting me know what month and year we bought the book. My many years sitting behind the counter of the SU Bookshop allowed me to meet a vast array of Trinity students. And it was ultimately the idea of sharing these stories – the student-centric, realistic, tea-drinking, counter-leaning stories of the college I knew – that finally tempted me. I believed that by revealing the authentic tales of those who graced its cobbles from 2000 to 2010 we would open people's eyes to what real 'noughties' Trinity was like. This would be a Trinity less austere than the tourists' Trinity, but one that alumni might recognize more. The school librarian in me even hoped school-aged readers might see themselves in some of the contributors, opening Trinity up to those who might have otherwise dismissed it.

When Sorcha and I sat down to compile the list of potential contributors, we were united in our desire to represent a wide spectrum of campus life at the time. We asked our contributors to write as honestly as possible, and they obliged beautifully. Our writers dropped their masks and exposed vulnerabilities, opening up in a way we couldn't have predicted. It was clear that each person's Trinity, despite the overlap of time, was a different university, a different place. Contributors who I knew at the time – who I still know now – had huge, life-changing events that coloured their college experiences.

I loved being a Trinity student. Unlike many, my path to Trinity was an easy one. I grew up playing on the carpeted blocks in the foyer of the Department of Modern History and knew my way around campus as a teenager. I didn't question this advantage. I threw myself into every aspect of student life – writing for *Trinity News* (later defecting to the *University Record*), managing Trinity FM and taking up all sorts of Students' Union positions. Of course it caught up with me later, but that's a different tale.

Recalling old memories and contacting Trinity friends and connections for this project has been a happy experience. For some it might not have been so easy. To our contributors, thank you for your openness and willingness to share your stories. I have had many lovely interactions by email, phone and Zoom. You have all been so patient with us throughout the whole project.

And thank you to Sorcha: from the beginning, it has been comforting to have a co-editor with publishing experience, and one who attended Trinity in the second half of the decade. Meeting Sorcha in person added to my relief. From the beginning, our vision for the book aligned. If Sorcha had reservations about working with someone outside of publishing, she didn't let it show. I hope our vision for *Trinity Tales* has translated onto the page and that we have done justice to this project and to the stories shared by our contributors.

Katie Dickson

IN FEBRUARY 2019, an email appeared in my inbox inviting me to edit a collection of essays by Trinity graduates. It was not my first time hearing about the *Trinity Tales* collection – I had leafed through a copy of the 1970s edition I'd unearthed in my parents' living room a few months before, interested in reading a snapshot of what life on College Green was like three decades before I stepped through Front Arch.

Neither of my parents attended Trinity (although my dad did dream of going but missed out on the scholarship despite travelling from London in the spring of 1966 to sit the exam), and I didn't give it much thought during school. My plan was to study drama, become an actress and make it as a star on the Abbey, Gate and West End stages. This ambition did creep into my college years – I was never far from Players' Theatre during my time at Trinity – but I ended up studying for a degree in European Studies. For a curious, overly excitable, eager-to-do-everything-and-anything nineteen-year-old, it was the perfect choice.

Admittedly, Lilliput Press' request that I co-edit the latest collection of stories from former students gave me mixed feelings. I adored Trinity. I fell in love for the first time on the cobblestones of Front Square; I met fascinating, kind and talented people I'm lucky to still call my friends; I jetted away to Seville for a sun-soaked Erasmus programme in the south of Spain.

I also struggled with depression for the first time in my life during the whirlwind of First Year; I fell out of love and shed many tears over my on-again, off-again college boyfriend; I pitted myself against my highly intelligent classmates in European Studies only to fall to pieces, questioning my ability to do just about anything. I thrived off the unpredictability and erratic nature of college life. 2006–10 was an impulsive, intense and beautiful period in my life.

However, it took time for me to realize just how lucky I was to have this kind of university experience. The truth is, I have come to reflect on my undergraduate years with a tinge of unease. It was only after graduating, and leaving Dublin, that I started to properly appreciate the privilege I had enjoyed at that time.

I had been a middle-class Dublin girl, living at home, working as a waitress on the weekends in a popular Temple Bar restaurant, acting in plays, gigging and busking with friends, dining in apartments at Botany Bay, popping into the library for an occasional quick flick through a tome on the Spanish Civil War or the French Revolution. I didn't have to pay bills, and our annual fees – the so-called student 'contribution' payment – were a meagre €700 when compared to the €3,000 plus Irish students pay today for 'free' third-level education.

I wasn't involved in student politics and only briefly dipped my toes into student journalism in my final few months before graduation. I was aware of the financial chaos unfolding in the world around me but chose to hide away in the comfort of Players' front of house.

I knew I was the stereotypical Trinity student and became uncomfortable with that label, particularly given the route my work took in the years that followed, meeting and interviewing people from some of Ireland's most marginalized and forgotten communities. I reflected on my college years with great fondness, but a big part of me wanted to go back and give my 21-year-old self a good talking to. A reminder to open my eyes and take stock of the diversity all around me.

Because, contrary to popular belief, Trinity was slowly but steadily diversifying in the first decade of the 2000s. Yes, it was still predominantly white, and its student body included some of the wealthiest people I'd ever met. But I also had classmates who relied on scholarships to make it through to Final Year and who worked long hours to cover rent and food. I met students who had made it in through the invaluable Trinity Access Programme (TAP) which, as you will read from this collection, really does transform people's lives.

And so I embarked on editing this collection in large part to give a platform to these voices – the people in Irish society who may not immediately connect to the privilege associated with Trinity College. The finished book is a fusion of voices – male, female, black, white, gay, straight, middle-class, working-class, Irish, Nigerian, Welsh, Iraqi, Canadian.

I owe huge thanks to my co-editor Katie Dickson for the brilliant contributors she sourced from the early years of the 2000s, and, more importantly, for her support and friendship as we worked through this project. When we first started on the book, we met in bustling coffeeshops to chat through plans, blissfully unaware that these real-life catch-ups would abruptly come to an end in March 2020. The bulk of the work on this book was done remotely, via Zoom and email, at a time when we were both struggling emotionally and psychologically with the burden of COVID-19. I think we held each other together on this project during that time, so thank you, Katie.

Most importantly, thank you to the writers. Your willingness to generously give up your time to reflect on your college years and bring your voice to this collection is hugely appreciated. Thanks to your hard work, we have produced what I believe to be an original and insightful chronicle of how it felt to study at Trinity during the first decade of the twenty-first century. Go raibh míle maith agaibh.

Sorcha Pollak

Katie Dickson. Photo credit: Lee Carroll.   *Sorcha Pollak. Photo credit: Waleed Safi.*

THE FUTURE WAS INFINITE

jarlath gregory

IT WAS A NEW MILLENNIUM, and nothing had changed – yet. The academic year at Trinity began the same way it always did. As you approached the great wooden gates, the hustle and bustle of city-centre living fell away, only to be replaced with the rush of new faces at Freshers' Week. You passed through Front Arch, its wooden floor littered with flyers, as representatives of the various student societies thrust drinks vouchers, membership cards and goodie bags in your bewildered face. A mixture of conservative, trendy, plain, extravagant, avant-garde and downright weird-looking young people went about their business, flurrying along in a whirl of scarves and satchels, boots and bicycles, cliques and camaraderie. Being in Trinity always felt as if you were a world removed from the commerce and commotion of Ireland's capital city. The clamorous bodies belonging to the Phil and the Hist were always up early, bagging the best booths right inside the archway, and clobbering the fresh crop of unsuspecting youth with promises of the biggest events and most extravagantly wine-soaked after-parties, all of which were true. Still, the most important thing was to find your tribe, and there were plenty to discover – faultlessly polite Christians and Muslims; enthusiastic foodies and impassioned environmentalists; Trinity Players and rugby players; the long-standing Literary Society and the recently revived Lesbian,

Gay and Bisexual Society, which was constantly in the process of debating a name change.

Pre-social media, debates about transgender inclusion or reclaiming the word 'queer' had not yet hit the toxic court of public opinion. While it was generally felt that we should provide the widest possible rainbow umbrella for all those who weren't straight and our allies, the LGB Society had plenty of earnest discussions in House 6, where we shared a room with the Socialist Workers' Party, about whether becoming the LGBT or Queer Society would help or hinder our chances of acquiring student funding or drinks sponsorship. We might not have been the largest society, but if we weren't throwing the coolest parties, who were we?

Although it was a watershed time for queer identities, the closet was deep and solid. My friend Ronan, as well as being in the LGB Soc, was also a member of Young Fine Gael, and was particularly impressed with two other students making waves in the party at the time. 'Leo Varadkar and Lucinda Creighton, watch out for them in the future. They won't be joining the LGB Soc any time soon, though.' Meanwhile, we were more concerned about garnering publicity for National Coming Out Day than dreaming about same-sex marriage, and more worried about winning the on-campus debates – for example, 'Is camp holding back gay rights?', with a strong turn by Panti Bliss – than wondering if we should be debating our rights as opposed to demanding them. There was groundwork to do in both raising awareness and winning the argument about gay rights in our own personal lives before we could even imagine the debate reaching national proportions. I did a year as the LGB Rights Officer, and although I only dealt with a few incidents of students struggling with their identity, the Students' Union Council did spend hours debating whether or not access to information about abortion services should continue freely, largely due to a duly elected but fervently Catholic minority opinion. Although it felt as though the arguments around queer rights were at a tipping point of wider acceptance, the activism was nascent and slipped easily between the personal and political. Other debates, although no less fiercely contested, were up against more entrenched views, with rather more organizational opposition.

It was also at this time that I signed a book deal for my first novel, *Snapshots*, which I'd been working on with more dedication than I gave to my actual studies. The first draft was rough in some places and highly polished in others, the result of many all-nighters in the twenty-four-hour computer labs in the Hamilton building, where I could be sure of enough privacy to turn hastily scribbled passages in notebooks into something resembling chapters. As befits its name, the novel was a patchwork of scenes from various perspectives, dropped into place to make overall narrative sense.

The novel gradually took shape in the underbelly of a gloomy concrete building lit by sickly strip-lighting and fuelled by vending-machine caffeine. It was a work in progress without direction for the longest time, existing somewhere between scribbles on foolscap and bytes on a floppy disk. My characters were real. Their voices were true. But, ultimately, what story were they living through?

I didn't have what you'd call a plot.

One night, when I'd emerged from the subterranean hum of the labs to walk home alone through campus on a cool, clear night, the end scene came to me with the clarity of mind that only materializes when you allow yourself to stop overthinking whatever problem it is you're working on. I paused outside the Berkeley, scratched the bones of it on a page and went home content. With the ending in sight, I could work backwards, follow the narrative thread from action to consequence to what was now, with an obviousness that made me wonder why it had taken me so long to see it, the only, inevitable conclusion.

I'd been to some Lit Soc events, mostly for the free booze. The smart money was on Belinda McKeon, who as well as being a famous beauty on campus was also known to be serious about her writing. Still, amongst the various literary types I'd met a friendly girl called Sharon who'd told me that Lilliput Press were actively looking for edgy fiction, so why not send my manuscript to them? At the time, it felt urgent to write queer voices. In a mainstream environment brimming with stories of how the boom was affecting the marriages, mortgages, kids and careers of straight couples, queer lives were still considered edgy, and were largely underexplored in popular culture. The challenge then was that queer voices were rarely recognized or promoted at all. The challenge now, in a culture in which being queer is no longer remarkable, is that queer voices are not often recognized as being distinctly different from the mainstream, or promoted as worthy of celebration in their own right. For better or worse, we've largely returned to being the supporting characters in straight drama.

It was also a world in which the internet had not yet become ubiquitous. The only people who understood internet culture were nocturnal geeks who played violent online video games in twenty-four-hour net cafés. The computer rooms in Trinity were constantly host to classes for those struggling to make the leap from handwritten to printed essays. There was never a queue for the Mac labs, as Apple technology, in a world before iPhones, was as mysterious and unfathomable as the rules of a foreign country. Other people were at home there, you could stick your nose in the door and you might even clumsily pass an afternoon there yourself – but you could never truly be one of them. It was not unusual to see queues for a payphone, with one frantic student thumbing coin after coin into the machine, while others stood behind her, resigned to waiting or ostentatiously checking their watches. Mobile phones were only just beginning to make the transition from overpriced status symbol to workaday necessity. I remember sitting outside the Arts Block with my friend Vinnie, a successful web entrepreneur, who confidently predicted that the next generation of mobile phones would have built-in cameras.

Built-in cameras! I almost spat out my coffee.

Pre-social media, books went out into the world off their own bat, as did students, for the most part. There was less awareness of having a personal brand, and very little chance of either building a devoted following or being widely vilified online. Print media held all the sway, as alternative routes to success were so far largely theoretical – in fact, some would have said heretical, as the highly canonized establishment of Sunday supplements and glossy magazines seemed inalienable. Reputations, popular opinions and received wisdom rose and fell on the say-so of journalists, not Twitter followers or Instagram likes. We spent an inordinate amount of money on CDs, and – perhaps because you invested so much spare cash in keeping up with pop culture – the music you bought really mattered. Music was your tribe, and dictated the clothes you wore, the haircut you sported, the pubs you frequented – in short, your clique.

In the 90s, you couldn't go wrong with Radiohead. Everyone desperately wanted to like the abstract new direction of *Kid A* but couldn't quite manage to, so you had to pick the background soundtrack to your impromptu student dinner parties wisely, mindful of the tribes you found yourself having to accommodate. It was either pasta, pesto and a few cans if you'd been caught off-guard and had to throw something together at the last minute (in which case, someone always came armed with a copy of Coldplay's *Parachutes*, an inoffensive crowd-pleaser), or Thai green chicken curry and a bottle of wine looted from your last drinks reception if you wanted to impress (in which case, P.J. Harvey's *Stories From the City, Stories From the Sea* was both credible and accessible, and wouldn't upset your guests – at least, not until Thom Yorke's guest appearance). Either way, your Britney Spears single of *Oops … I Did It Again* stayed safely hidden until everyone was drunk and you wanted to go out, or, worse again, everyone remained sober and you wanted to get rid of them.

When I think back to Trinity in the noughties, the one thing that stands out more truly than anything else is the lifelong friendships made and forged there. Perhaps because it was pre-social media you had to make an actual, physical effort to keep up with the people with whom you wanted to stay in touch. No matter how hungover the morning, no matter how late the day's lectures began, lunchtime was sacrosanct. A gang of us – Colin, Arlene and me – would scrape ourselves together and meet our friend Trish in the Arts Block. It was the best place to people-watch and peruse the posters for upcoming events, and then make our way to Trish's rooms to dissect the latest Belle and Sebastian album, last night's drunken shenanigans or Samuel Irons's hair (he was a big deal in the Arts Block). There were sandwiches in greaseproof paper and endless pots of tea. There was gossip about who kissed whom, and where. There were afternoon pints in the Buttery and days upon days to regret it afterwards, after throwing up in someone else's sink, and somehow crawling in to your 9 am seminar – *rude* – to at least show your face for the compulsory subjects.

Crucially, and in a way that is possibly different to student life today, there was optimism for the future. It was a time when decent jobs were relatively easy to come by, whether you'd been to college or not. Positive progressive politics were on the rise. Rent had not become crippling. The world was not on fire. It was possible to chuck in a job that had become stale or move abroad without much of a plan, simply to try something new or see what happened next, because making things up as you went along was a valid life option, and there was room for failure along the way.

My happiest memory is walking through the grounds of Trinity after lunch with Colin, Arlene and Trish, wrapped up against the springtime chill, drifting by the Campanile, the buildings of Front Square crisply cut against the radiant blue sky. There was nothing special about the day, save a deep contentment with my lot in the world, and a feeling that the future was infinite.

But like the ending of novels, and the rise of technology, and the songs that come to define an era, and the vagaries of the ever-changing political landscape, some things only seem inevitable in retrospect. The future was ours to be written, and Trinity was offering us permission.

Jarlath Gregory (centre) with Trish Brazil and Arlene Crummy at The Buttery Bar *during the Trinity Ball, 2000. Photo credit: Colin Crummy.*

Jarlath Gregory (TCD 1997–2001, Sociology and Social Policy; 2016–17, MPhil in Creative Writing) is from Crossmaglen, Northern Ireland, and lives in Stoneybatter, Dublin. He is the author of **Snapshots, G.A.A.Y.**, **The Organised Criminal** and most recently **What Love Looks Like**, his first Young Adult novel, released March 2021 by O'Brien Press.

ROCKING THE DELICATELY BALANCED CHARADE

sallay matu-garnett (loah)

'AND THERE was nothing to fear, and nothing to doubt.'

Radiohead's lyrics reverberating throughout the Trinity Exam Hall, a frisson of tense expression right the way up my back, the sound waves emerging from *my* mouth. The year of Our Lord 2010. This was the moment I decided I would turn my back on all I had promised to my future and become that most commonplace of rudimentary magicians: a singer.

I spent four years in the late 2000s studying pharmacy at Trinity College. By anyone's standards, I had made the most sensible choice any bright-eyed millennial could make. I grew up with two parents from different countries and cultures, always travelling between the suburbs of Kildare and two capital cities in West Africa: Banjul and Freetown. By eighteen, I wanted stability, responsibility and a useful body of knowledge. I wanted to stay put!

I had loved biochemical sciences in school but missed the marks for medicine by a hair's breadth due to unforeseen chaos during my Leaving Cert year. Pharmacy reared its head as the obvious choice, one line of a CAO form above music. After a post-school 'gap year' (a term now made infamous by the supposed ludicrous privilege needed to take one, and the stereotypes that have been created by those who do), I walked through the College Green archway and into those hallowed halls ready for all my wildest expectations to be fulfilled.

Let me be clear and profoundly honest: those expectations were by no means modest. I never intended to go to Trinity and not become a 'Trinner'. On the contrary, that was my primary aim. I wanted every scrap of Trinity prestige going. I had always been academically ambitious and I wanted to win at everything. I had also sacrificed a social life as a teen to achieve those academic capabilities, so I wanted to fix that by being present everywhere and being friends with everyone. I wanted the glamour of all things genteel to rub off on me. I wanted to sit hungover in drab rented rooms or grand, fabulous ones watching old movies. I wanted my vistas filled with cobblestones, columns and gothic windows. I wanted to speak in modernist poetic cadences and I wanted to get wasted at the Pav. I wanted to join 101 societies and I wanted to fall in love 101 times. I wanted to play jazz and I wanted to play classical music. I wanted to do yoga and I wanted to be carried home. I wanted to sing at student balls and I wanted there to be enough chaos to cry at parties. I wanted to never need to sleep. I wanted to be wealthy, successful and free. I wanted to be happy. I wanted to have a great future.

I did a great deal of those things, a great many more, and attempted to do them all simultaneously. Those years were a gift. And, like any gift from the gods, it could not be returned. In the doing of everything under the College Green sun, I lost myself. I was a student living on grants that my patient, loving, single mother had helped me secure, so that her daughter – born into poverty but reared through hard work into the middle class, and who was fiercely demanding of life and greedy for every experience – could fill her appetite for knowledge. I worked several jobs in the summers, at home and abroad, collecting savings and languages. In the winters I went snowboarding with my fabulous friends and tried to keep up on the slopes while simultaneously trying to keep up with pharmaceutics.

In the first year, I tried to leave pharmacy, knowing I probably, maybe, didn't really want to be a pharmacist and therefore ought not to waste everyone's time. I wanted to be an *artiste*, experience everything and then write about it all. However, there was no plan of how I'd go about doing this. I did, after all, want to be a useful citizen, and an artist with no plan is not very useful to anyone, least of all themselves. So, a friend and my college tutor talked me out of my storm-out, and I reconsidered. I committed, renamed as what I felt was the more suave 'Apothecary' class, made football team names like *Bend It Like Benzene* and just got on with it. (At no point in my life since have I ever regretted this decision, though I did leave pharmacy eventually. The stability and sense of confidence that comes from being of service has been profoundly necessary to my character and indeed my mental health.) Like any half-decent committed footballer, I knew if my jersey was still clean by the end, I hadn't played hard enough.

I failed an exam for the first time in the midst of the maelstrom of heartbreak. I went to a therapist for the first time when I kept crying for 'no reason' in laboratories and libraries. There were club nights. There were choral masses. Front Square was the scene of many a Trinity Ball crime, many a term-time conversation and the ultimate moment of anticlimactic release at graduation. I lived in a Georgian house on Raglan Road with my best friend and I sang jazz standards every week on Westland Row with the best musos. I played the violin and surfed and read and ate Tesco frozen pizzas. My sweethearts made me mixtapes to soundtrack our ferocious, possessive, youthful love. The fervour and ecstasy, combined with a wild swing from unbounded joy to total despair, exposed deep inner anxieties from a childhood of uncertainty and a fearful dread that all good things must end.

And end they did. Bang smack in the middle of my degree, the 2008 financial crisis *occurred*. We heard of older siblings or parents of people we knew having salaries slashed and losing their jobs, business and homes. The dark cloud of the burst economic bubble moved across the waters of our collective consciousness. Suddenly the prospects of a life that sounded as breezy as the chorus of every Thrills song was no more. Bertie Ahern went from being 'the Taoiseach who drank at the Quill pub in Drumcondra near our mates' flat' to the sinister overlord of our generation's demise. We were waking up to the end of an era of excess and the end of the *Twilight* novel series. What was to become of us all?

Even though the pandemic of recession was changing the fabric of society, I felt strangely cushioned by the institution surrounding me, along with also getting to spend a semester of my third year on Erasmus in Montpellier. The dream persisted: I had a minuscule and totally lovable rectangular pod room in a student dorm. I drank rosé, sang in the labs, sang in the jazz clubs and learned that French pharmacies at the time sold the highest number of antidepressants and slimming products in Europe. Being transported to a city with one of the oldest European medical schools and one of the youngest age demographics was the best and arguably most sensible form of escapism for a still-green young'un. Not yet ready to fully fly the Trinity nest, I found a semester to be more than enough time to soak in cosy, reassuring French bureaucracy, education and the Beaujolais festival. Not enough time to miss home. Enough of a break from the growing tension of approaching the educational finish line in the midst of an economic downturn. *Alors, on danse.*

Returning home after those few months in France, I resolved to squeeze every last blessing I could out of the remaining time. I had not shaken off that strange, unresolved dread but was determined to move forward through hyperactivity and the deranged pursuit of everything that made me 'happy'. I can only presume, from the biased view that is memory, that to everyone near to me – family, friend and foe – I was both utterly charming and utterly unbearable.

Be that as it may, by the end of Third Year, the inner gnawing of being out of place and the fear for our collective future was getting louder. I was so involved and so present, yet sometimes I would secretly sleep for days and tell everyone that I was with other people. Flaky was my student name, number and address. I was popular, yet the crippling loneliness I felt regularly drove me at best to write terrible poetry, or at worst to seek help from dangerous thought patterns.

The one thing that persistently grounded me in those years of ferocious overactivity (covering this vague, growing sense of inadequacy to enter an uncertain world) was music. The orchestra rehearsals where I'd sit calmly in a second-violin desk quite literally soothed my nervous system. The gigs with the lads and our dear, sweet soul–funk–jazz band Jazzberries (oh, the frivolous titles of youth) hunkered me back to the moment and a sense of fleeting purpose and FUN. To this day, there are chords we sang in a Polish choral piece in Singers that I play to myself when the dung is really hitting the fan.

I am by nature cheerful, but deeper psychological issues were beginning to surface and affect the delicately balanced charade. My colour, this 'blackness', and how I interacted with the world because of it, was leading to uncomfortable questions, in brief moments of mental quiet, for which I had no answers. Womanhood and the sometime prison of its meaning was becoming undeniable: it was allowing me to start allowing myself to fail. By the time my final year came, it was clear that I was existing for what music was giving me and tolerating everything else. I was an exhausted, hyper-stimulated, undernourished life-junkie. That spring in 2010, I had friends asking whether I was OK, as I hadn't been to class in a couple of weeks. Enter, Radiohead.

When Rob Farhat and Brian Denvir, my dear friends in the orchestra, asked if I would put the violin down and sing two Radiohead songs at the concert of homegrown arrangements they were organizing for us, I set about immediately to find a singing coach. I might have been in final year, I might have been clinically malnourished and depressed, but I wasn't screwing up *Radiohead*. And then I discovered Judith Mok. A friend's mum, her reputation preceded her. Legend had it she had coached *the* Thom Yorke during the recording of the album *Hail to the Thief*. Completely out of my price range or my professional capabilities, I nonetheless convinced her to take me on for a few weeks for this most crucial of engagements.

Suddenly, I had a reason to wake up in the morning. That eleven-beat long note wasn't going to learn to sing itself. I needed to start meditating again, because how else would I convey the depth of transcendence of Yorke's phrasing? I felt I should probably start eating properly too because vocalists couldn't faint onstage, it hadn't been in vogue for centuries.

The lessons with Judith were (and still are) intense, focused and purposeful. Everything I had always wanted and sought, but for the exact end I had been lacking all that time: to create the perfection of the sound wave emerging from one's body. Around lesson 3, I had the fabled 'cry' many of her early students experience, the surrendering to what feels like life's real work. Those few weeks set in motion a sea change.

Though I trained fully and worked as a chemist, it wasn't long before I left my first job to dream and to plan a life in music. Though I had always written songs, there was now a sense of meaning and momentum. I could comb apart each line with Judith and excavate profundity in the most humble of lyrics. To surrender to the arts is to hold hands with the humility of the beginner's mind.

There is always more to know and to express and always someone better than you. Infinite homework for the rudimentary magician. Yet in that, there is the potential for infinite satisfaction.

Ten years later, when I watch back over the grainy footage from that 2010 Radiohead show, I find holes in my technique, I hear mistakes. It is not necessarily as magical as it felt. I can see my discomfort in myself. I remember the nervousness beforehand in the side room of the Exam Hall chatting to Pats (now I Have a Tribe). I had done so many gigs and been tested in that Exam Hall so many times, but I knew this was different. I knew I had found, or rather accepted, my calling in the most roundabout of ways. The future was finally starting.

Photo credit: Abe Neihum.

Sallay-Matu Garnett (Loah) (TCD 2006–10; Pharmaceutical Sciences) is an artist and performer of Irish and Sierra Leonean origins who grew up between Kildare and West Africa. She has worked and performed with Lisa Hannigan, Kíla, Hozier, Cassandra Wilson, the Wainwrights, Paul Brady and Bilal. In 2019, Garnett starred as Mary Magdalene in Andrew Lloyd Webber and Tim Rice's **Jesus Christ Superstar** at the Barbican in London, and she has multiple television and film appearances to her name (**Striking Out, Finding Joy, Girl from Mogadishu**).

FOR THE FIRST TIME IN MY LIFE, I FELT ALIVE

katriona o'sullivan

SHE IS ACTUALLY speaking to ME … in Latin! As I stand in front of Mary Robinson, one of the few Irish presidents I actually know of and admire, it finally feels like I belong. Trinity College is finally acknowledging me. After nine years of hard study, loneliness, sadness and immense joy, I'm part of this place. I turn around with my PhD certificate and see my beautiful boy Sean and Dave, his dad, looking on with pride. Sean really has no clue what the hell this all means but he smiles anyhow.

I have to start my Trinity Tale at the end. If I'd started at the beginning, you'd probably have stopped reading. You may have thought you'd picked up a copy of *Take a Break* or *Woman's Way* by mistake. You see, I am not your usual TCD graduate. There are no doctors, lawyers or graduates in my recent family … 'Katriona O'Sullivan PhD' wouldn't have really fitted on my social welfare card or my lone parents benefit book.

I'm what is commonly known as an 'access' student; I come from an 'under-represented student group'. I am a charity case, an experiment. I am one of the students that was allowed in because someone fought hard against the elite education system that believes intelligence is measured by school performance.

Someone recognized that people like me also had the potential to be people like you.

Before I jump onto my soapbox, let me explain. I grew up in a family that most people would consider 'disadvantaged'. My parents were heroin addicts, my dad spent a lot of time in prison and I had little or no support from within or outside my family home. I watched my mam inject drugs and helped her smuggle drugs into my dad in jail. I was a child that you would have pitied, the child that is talked about in shocking newspaper stories. Despite my family drama, and the regular hunger pains, I was bright and vivacious. I loved school, I loved to learn, I read avidly. I was excellent at all sports and was, and still am, extremely determined. But when you live in a family that does not aspire to much, and you are surrounded by people who cannot see past your disadvantage, it's really hard to dream big. I knew no one who went to university or college and dreamed of being somewhere else or someone else. I didn't dream of a university education or travelling the world – it only stretched as far as being on TV or becoming a pop star.

In secondary school my life began to spiral. It became more and more difficult for me to get up, to respond appropriately, to smile or even to try. I could no longer ignore the loneliness I felt, and when I hit fifteen I fulfilled the destiny my upbringing offered and got pregnant. The shame of becoming a 'gym slip mum' meant I could not face school and left. When I was six months' pregnant I was asked to leave my family home and ended up homeless. We squatted in flats and eventually I ended up in a homeless hostel for young mothers where my son was born. I tried to focus on him, getting my welfare payments, securing a corporation house and being like every other girl in my situation. I worked hard at being the best I could be and made do.

Fast-forward seven years and I had achieved my all-time goal; I was a lone parent, I lived in a government-assisted flat in Dublin 1 and I was getting my social welfare. My child was doing his best and so was I. I had a cash-in-hand job cleaning Connolly Station. I woke at 6 am every morning, leaving my son John in bed while I walked to the station and cleaned the dirtiest office you have ever seen in your life. I had it all. But still, I couldn't shake the feeling of 'is this really it?'

THE TRINITY ACCESS PROGRAMME

'Why do you want to do this course?' the interviewer asks me. He seems nice, but I'm sure he can see through me. 'I want to change my life,' I reply. 'I feel like I'm missing something.' He smiles, and I'm sure I've said something wrong. 'Do you read books?' he asks. 'Yes,' I say. 'I have always loved to read.' He smiles again and makes a note.

I applied to the Trinity Access Programmes on a whim. My friend Karen had told me she was studying Law in Trinity College and, like me, she had kids and was on her own. She struggled like me and, more importantly, she spoke like me. When she said she'd gotten into this big, posh college through TAP I was excited and envious. I didn't think you were allowed in through the main gates. The only people I knew who went in there were going to rob bikes. Now here I was, sitting in front of three people, trying to convince them to let me into a programme that would help me become something I wasn't sure I even wanted to be.

When the letter arrived offering a place on the access programme, my dad got it framed. I felt happy, sad, scared and hopeful. But who would help me, who would look after my son? My friends were supportive, and one of them told me about the Vinnies (St Vincent de Paul) – a group who could help people like me. I called the number, trying to explain without sounding desperate. They came over and were kind. A little posh, but they seemed genuine. I felt ashamed, but they didn't seem to judge me. They reminded me of the teachers who reached out to me when I was younger, or the kind lady in our local shop who would give me food because she knew I was hungry. They told me to relax, that they would help. They paid for my childcare.

The first day of TAP was strange. I had brought my new notepad, pens and a few highlighters like a good student. We were located in Goldsmith Hall at the back of campus – you didn't even have to go through the main gates to get there. I met the other students, we were all so diverse. I was the youngest mature student at twenty-three; there was even a lady aged sixty on the course. We were all so different, yet there was a camaraderie there, a sense of belonging. We came from different backgrounds – not everyone had a history of neglect or deprivation. Some people were migrants, others were mature students who worked in trades or were builders. Some were housewives. There were school-leavers too – young people from deprived or DEIS schools who were challenged by the education system but showed potential.

We formed groups, the young matures and the old matures, the gothy kids and the Tallaght heads. I didn't really get into a group, I had no time to socialize and had to care for my son on my own. I also felt awkward and still felt ashamed. I don't know why, but I've always felt like this, so making friends – trusting people – didn't happen easily. Irena, the course director, liked me, I could tell. She kept checking on me and smiling when I looked her way – she made me feel at home. We started TAP by doing taster classes – two weeks to decide whether you wanted to be a science, social science or arts student. I knew I loved books, so English seemed like a given. Biology, physics, chemistry, philosophy, psychology – I loved everything. I sat drinking in the knowledge and, for the first time in my life, I felt alive. I mean, really alive.

Everything I was learning felt so new and exciting. I remember sitting in the psychology class with Professor Ray Fuller thinking, 'This guy is amazing.' He talked about his family while showing us examples of behaviourism, and I was hooked. I decided to focus on English, Philosophy, Psychology and Law as my four subjects, and also took study skills and maths as core subjects. Maths was my biggest challenge. I hate being slow to learn anything. I had always been someone who picked things up easy. Maths was not one of those things. I spent the whole year fighting with our maths teacher, but if I wanted to choose Psychology for my degree I had to do higher-level maths in TAP, and this scuppered me. But I found my way. My friend Liviu – another mature student who was excellent at maths – tutored me and reminded me it was going to be OK.

One thing that is overlooked when we consider TAP students is our resilience. I know how to survive, and that is a skill. I used it to survive maths and have used it many times since. I used my capacity to challenge, to fight and to ask for help to get me through. TAP became a home for me. Irena was my guide, I could tell her anything. The ladies in the office, Sheila and Elaine, provided more care. They helped with finances, books, laptops and also gave hugs, relationship advice and so much more. TAP wasn't just about education, it was about belonging, belief and care. I grew there and started to believe in me. My essays were good, and my work got better. I learned what I liked, what I hated, what I needed to improve. I learned that I was good enough. I still doubt that, though.

The April before my TAP exams, I received the offer of a degree place in Trinity. I was lucky enough to be offered my first three choices: Psychology, Philosophy and BESS. I just needed to pass my exams to progress. But I wobbled and decided I couldn't do it, that it was too much. I didn't belong, and I stopped attending. Before you judge me for this, you have to remember that success isn't easy for someone like me. I was used to failing or feeling bad. So feeling good and hopeful wasn't easy to accept – self-sabotage is normal for many like me. This is where TAP came to the rescue. Irena literally dragged me by the scruff of the neck into my exams – she made me see the worth I had and the life I could have. Without TAP, I would not be here today. Without the opportunity to breathe in knowledge, to step slowly into this beautiful place, into Trinity, I would have never been able to succeed. I see TAP as the secure base from which I was able to navigate my educational path. It was and is always there for me to return to.

GOING TO BIG SCHOOL – TRINITY FOR REAL

'Now you all know the equation of the line so I won't go over this for you.' My first lecture as an undergrad in Trinity Psychology is statistics. I am sure I will fail. I don't know the equation of the line. I didn't even finish my secondary schooling, let alone memorize the equation of a line. Shit, I shouldn't have come here. As I look around, this feeling mounts. They all look so confident. They dress weird too, like they have money but no money. Messy clothes that are designer brands. I have on fake tan and a hun-bun. I don't belong here.

Those first few months in Trinity proper were hard. I felt lost; the Psychology class was small, which meant I couldn't hide. I was sitting with really middle-class kids who had got around 580 points in their Leaving Cert, and I felt like a failure. Two years before I started my degree, I had been working as the dinner lady in the Institute of Education. I served sausage rolls to the students who could afford grind schools. On the second day of my Psychology degree, a girl came up and asked if I remembered her. She had dreadlocks and was really well-spoken, Sorcha was her name. I said, 'Sorry, no.' She said she had been in Fifth Year at the Institute when I was working there, and that I had served her lunch for the year – I was mortified. She was very polite and said, 'Fair play to you,' but I immediately felt ashamed again.

I spent a good proportion of my time as a Trinity undergraduate rotating between feeling ashamed of my past and proud of myself for being there. Once I got used to the lectures, I excelled in my classes. I wasn't the usual mature student who asked a million questions, but I was well able to suss out who I needed to know. I never asked for an extension in my four years, I never missed a deadline or an exam. I passed everything I sat – even in Second Year when I gave birth to my second son in February. I didn't defer, and I sat my exams in May when Sean was just two months old. I was determined, resilient and driven. I had no clue what my plans were for after, but I knew I loved learning.

The psychology lecturers were fantastic, they were so kind and caring. Even the nerdy ones who were biology focused and seemed like they had no social skills – if you approached them, they loved to talk about their research and wanted to help. I learned so much from my degree. I learned about how a child develops, about the power of attachment and love. I learned how to think critically and how to be a better student. But, while I am outgoing, I didn't mix well. My life outside college didn't bode well for trips to the pub with the other students. But learning was enough for me.

CLASS REP

'I nominate Katriona for this, she knows everything, and is not afraid to speak her mind.' It's Second Year and the psychology class are nominating a class rep who can represent them at staff meetings. I look around, I see nodding heads. I smile and think to myself, 'They are nominating me as class rep. I swear a lot and still dress like a chav, but they see me.' It feels good.

I was elected class rep and became the go-to person for the students. I started to make friends. I was still cagey and did not let too many people in, but I met some really lovely people. I learned that life was hard for all of us. One of the students, Amy, was so kind to me. She was the star of our year, always achieving high grades and succeeding. But she also helped me, and I learned a lot from her. I discovered people who have had privileged lives are lovely too. They were not all judging me – or, if they were, they did it politely and hid it well. I met other great people in my year – Conor, Jen, Milena – who shared the troubles of college with me. While the bond wasn't as strong with them as with my own people, I started to belong. Or maybe I just started to not care so much.

In the background to all this, I knew I always had TAP to return to. Whenever I was stuck for money or support, or whenever I doubted myself, I could pop over to Goldsmith Hall and find a friendly face. It wasn't the big army it is now, we all knew each other. I also got to know the supports in Trinity too. Helen Richardson in grad studies was my go-to person. She worked then as admin for the senior tutor, but I knew I could pop in for a chat or to ask advice on money or just college life. By the end of Third Year, I had found my feet. While I would never fully belong in TCD, I knew by then I was good enough. I got to know all the catering staff, all the cleaners and all the builders during my nine years as a student and three years as staff. These were and still are my people. As a research student, I began to flourish, and by the end of Third Year I was achieving high 2.1s for all my work and felt confident I would pass my degree.

RESULTS

'The results will be posted online in June. If you guys are thinking about using this degree for anything decent in the future, a 2.1 or above is your only hope.' She smiles as she says this. Does she not understand that I have sons at home? I am trying my fucking best, don't tell me that even that will be not enough! I put my head down and work harder than I have worked before. If I fail at this I am fucked, all of this will have been for nothing.

I'll never forget the day the results were posted on that noticeboard. Back then, a list of student numbers appeared in the order of grades, so you could see who got firsts, 2.1s, etc. I remember standing in the small reception area of the first floor of Áras an Phiarsaigh, absolutely terrified. When the page went up everyone seemed very demure, checking their grades and walking away. No one was talking about their results or letting anything out. When I got to the board, I started from the bottom, running my finger up the sheet. I wasn't in the fails, phew. I wasn't in the 2.2s – yeah! I looked at the 2.1s, expecting to see my number, but it wasn't there. Then I saw my student number listed in the first-class honour section and let out a massive scream. I was like, 'Yes, fucking yes,' I couldn't hold it in.

David Hevey came out of his office at the noise and smiled broadly. 'I am delighted for you, Katriona,' he said. I told everyone, I was like a child. I knew it wasn't very humble, but I had worked my ass off to get there and I felt so proud of myself and my family. I walked off delighted. I was offered a PhD studentship that summer and began my PhD studies in the TCD Psychology department pretty much straight away. Once you get into TCD, you often don't want to leave. It felt so beautiful and calm. But I didn't stay for the beauty, I stayed because it was the first place I actually realized my worth as a person, as a woman. Trinity College gave me an insight into my capabilities. It made me see the potential for my life and my family's life.

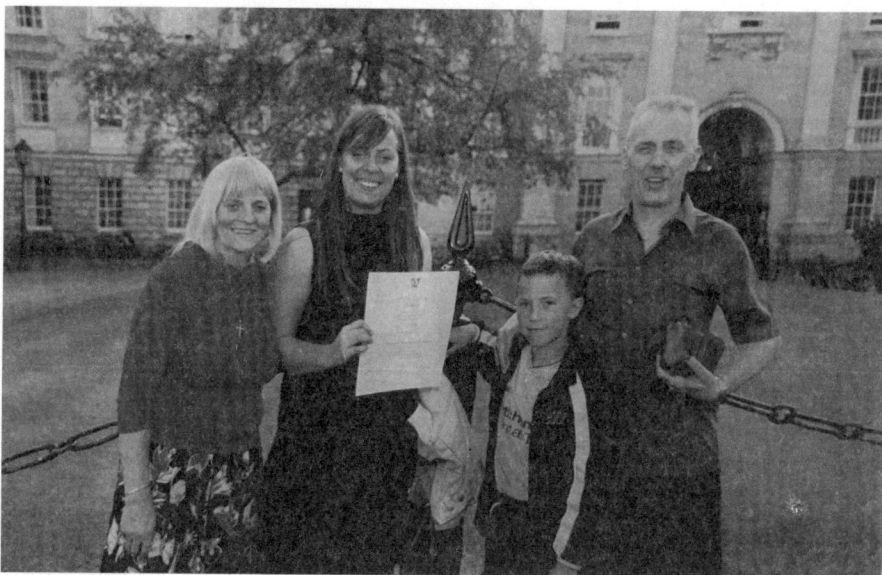

Katriona O'Sullivan with her parents, Tony and Tilly O'Sullivan, and her son John O'Sullivan in Front Square at her graduation from the Trinity Access Programme Foundation Course for Mature Students, 2003.

Dr Katriona O'Sullivan (TCD 2003, Trinity Access Programme Foundation Year; 2004–8, Psychology; 2008–12, PhD Psychology) is a Lecturer in the Department of Psychology and the ALL (Assisted Living and Learning) Institute at Maynooth University. She has published several papers on inclusion and secured significant funding to develop and research programmes which support equality and inclusion. She is an advocate for equality in education and talks openly about how her upbringing affected her opportunities to progress in life. With heroin addiction and crime being a part of her family history, Katriona has overcome significant challenges to achieve happiness and a healthy life.

SUCCESS IN FAILURE

kieran quinn

IT WAS almost like we were never supposed to succeed.

I remember striking up a conversation with a rugby-playing classmate of mine one evening during my first year at Trinity as we finished lectures.

'What are you up to?'

'Going training.'

'Oh me too – what time does yours start?'

'6.00.' (It was 5.30 now.)

'Oh. That's handy. Where do you train?'

'There.' He pointed to College Park, a one-minute walk from the Psychology building.

'Happy days,' I said, feeling genuinely chuffed for my classmate that he could basically roll out of class and onto his training ground. It wasn't until a few months later that I began to realize the significance of this. The easier it is to get to training, the more people want to go. And the more people that go training, the better your team is and the more chance you have of success.

On the other hand, I, newly up from Sligo, was heading out into the big, bad world of rush-hour Dublin to find a bus to Santry. And while I knew the capital city fairly well, it was very different when you were living there. Figuring out bus routes. Trying to be on time. And then there was cooking.

I remember one of the first nights in our flat when it was my turn to cook. I thought I knew how to rustle up a carbonara but ended up serving almost raw pasta with an uncooked egg drizzled over it with a few pieces of bacon scattered around. I managed to eat it, but when I arrived home later and the lads were sheepishly eating a takeaway I realized my culinary skills needed a bit of work.

But back to the famous bus to Santry. It was an education all in itself. Learning the hard way that if you didn't flag it down it wouldn't stop. Making your gear bag look as imposing as possible with the aim of keeping strangers out of the seat beside you. Clearing the condensation on the window in the vain hope of seeing some landmark, anything that would help you recognize your stop.

But I never did. I always missed it. One time the airplanes were so low above my head I thought I had somehow managed to get onto the runway at Dublin Airport. And so the commute became even longer. A walk to the bus, a wait, the interminable stop-start bus journey itself, the (now extended) walk to the pitch. Late for training. Again. How are you meant to figure this city out?

Meanwhile my rugby-playing colleague had finished training, and was in a warm shower looking forward to his dinner and maybe a few cans, and I hadn't even togged out.

But something kept me going back. It could have been the buzz of exercise. Or our football-mad manager Corkman Timmy Walsh who, despite everything, managed to prepare us extremely well for the on-field challenges we faced. The biggest attraction, however, was probably the chance to learn from and hang around with the older lads on the team. Lads from Kerry, Dublin, Laois, Derry – counties which unlike mine had actually tasted success at either underage or senior level during the previous years.

I went to the All-Ireland final in the summer of 2001 and saw one teammate – Niall Kelly – bomb a ball into the square from which Meath won a penalty. Another teammate, Alan Kerins, came on as a sub for Galway that day and won an All-Ireland medal. No one from Sligo has ever played in an All-Ireland final. But now I was playing with lads who had. And slowly but surely the realization came that I could hold my own with them. That there was no magic about these lads from more successful counties – they were just lads who loved playing football, like I was. The thing was, they had a bit more belief in themselves than I did.

And of course there was the craic. There was a trip in January of my first year to Ballinrobe to play IT Sligo, but the game was only a sideshow. The real reason for that journey was the night out. Those nights and those trips are etched in my memory. You never forget the buzz you get from feeling like you're part of the gang. You might not win much, but somehow that mattered less when there were others in the thick of it with you.

And people knew that. Especially Timmy. And the older lads on the team, the likes of John Teahan, Joe Mallon, Paul Kieran. These guys knew that if we were to have any chance, first we needed to attract and hold onto new players. Then we needed to forge a team spirit better than anything else out there.

And I began to feel like I could contribute. I played the full game that day in Ballinrobe, and after the match, when I was chatting to some clubmates from Sligo on the opposing team, I could tell they were surprised with how I did against them. A couple of weeks later I was named to start at midfield in the biggest game of the year – the first round of the Sigerson Cup. As a fresher. Ahead of big Joe Cullen who was in his final year. I felt like an impostor, but also knew I had to try and seize this opportunity.

Because the Sigerson Cup was where it was at. And even if you were good enough to make it through to the quarter-final, it meant you got to the Sigerson weekend – a crazy few days where the four quarter-finals were played on Friday, the two semi-finals on Saturday and the final on Sunday. But for a college footballer, this was where it was at. The pinnacle. The place to be.

But Trinity had never won it. The 1980–1 team had been the only one to reach a final, and while Joe Brolly and his team put the college on the map by winning two League titles a few years later, they lost three consecutive Sigerson semi-finals between 1989 and 1991, so the big prize still eluded us.

This year – my First Year, 1999–2000 – we were drawn away against 70 in the first round. A tough draw, whichever way you looked at it. UCC were second on the all-time Sigerson roll-of-honour, stacked with stars of recent Cork and Kerry underage teams. What's more, because of a quirky GAA rule, they were the reigning Cork and Munster club champions. Whichever way you looked at it, we were up against it.

It was a huge game, especially for our manager Timmy, who was leading his unfancied side to the Mardyke, one of the historic GAA venues in his native county. We didn't want to let him down. I especially wanted to justify his faith in me, especially when the easier and less risky call would have been to go with the older, more experienced player.

The game was nip and tuck all the way. It got more and more tense. I will never forget the electricity that ran through my body when we managed to draw level deep into the second half. I ran out to face the kickout, the surges of adrenalin making me feel that the ten minutes immediately ahead were more important than anything I had faced in my life so far. Unfortunately, a late goal swung it the way of our opponents and we lost by a point. Devastation all round, but honour in our performance.

In my second year we had a kinder draw, and we made it through to the quarter-final of the tournament in the spring of 2001 after wins over Dundalk IT and a star-studded Maynooth team. The lads were thrilled, as was Timmy. Even non-football people in college began to take an interest. The Sigerson weekend. What it was all about. And what's more, it was to be in Sligo that year. One weekend a friend from home showed me the programme that they had printed for the tournament – a who's who of county footballers from all around the country. And my name was among them.

And then some cows got sick.

The tournament was delayed and then delayed again. Eventually it was decided not to play it over the course of a weekend but in dribs and drabs here and there. We were drawn to play St Mary's University College from Belfast in Clones, and were nearly late for the game. The route our bus took meant we had to cross the border twice before going back into Co. Monaghan. Each time we had to disembark and disinfect. Our warm-up was a lot shorter than planned, we never got into the game and we were well beaten.

Third Year didn't go so well either, and Maynooth put us out of our misery by clinically exacting revenge on us for the previous year's defeat, beating us well in Santry.

And, all of a sudden, we were the senior players. While in a club or county team it takes ten to twelve years to go from being the youngest member of the team to one of the eldest, in college it takes just three. It was our time to lead.

The previous season had been poor, and before we broke up for the summer we had umpteen conversations, discussions, meetings, trying to figure out ways we could improve things. There was no county board, no club officers making decisions. It was a bunch of students calling the shots. For better or worse.

Everything was on the table. Training facilities, player intake, gear, sponsorship, even management. We approached the college authorities looking for some sort of use of college grounds for training but had no luck. They told us that with any sort of extra activity the condition of the grounds would deteriorate to a point where they wouldn't be usable for anyone.

That was OK – we took them at their word. But when there was no attempt to find any sort of a compromise, no attempt to work with us at all on our requests, we were made to feel firmly like second-class sporting citizens in our own college. We decided to focus elsewhere, raising some money to put towards scholarships and writing to secondary-school principals in the hope of attracting some of the best young talent in the country to Trinity.

The big call was the manager. Some lads began to voice the opinion that a change of management might not do us any harm. And while I could see the merit in this, I could also remember very clearly not only the faith shown in me by the man in question before the UCC game, but also the way in which he had helped a naïve and innocent young Sligo man to feel at home and settle into Dublin life.

A vote was held at the AGM and the result was decisive. I was tasked with the job of ringing Timmy to tell him that we had decided to go in a different direction the following season. I remember it clear as daylight: aged twenty-two, armed with a can of Bavaria for some literal Dutch courage, standing on the grass outside the Pav, telling Timmy Walsh over the phone we had decided that he wasn't going to be the manager anymore.

I'm sure it was difficult for Timmy, but in fairness to him he remained civil throughout and didn't seem to hold anything against me on the few occasions we met after that.

But summer came and went, and after all our planning and meetings, we still had no manager, until one of Joe Brolly's old teammates Cian Murtagh approached a friend of his about the job. At the end of September, Cavan man Vincent Kelly rode into town, dust flying in his wake.

The following year was wonderful. Vincent was a larger-than-life character, and what he lacked in managerial experience he certainly made up for in terms of enthusiasm, commitment and generosity (of time and money). He genuinely believed that we were going to win the Sigerson Cup. And we grew to believe it too. After three fairly heavy colours match defeats to UCD in previous years, it was great to finally get one over on them this time, and we celebrated like we had won the entire competition.

Soon it was Sigerson time again, and a few weeks later we arrived at the grounds of Dublin superclub St Vincents for the first round, getting another reminder of what proper facilities looked like. Sadly, just like three years previously in the Mardyke, we had a heroic and narrow loss to one of the tournament favourites. We were never going to win the game with just eight points, and even though we limited DCU to 1–7, once again the goal made all the difference, and we exited the competition. Some of us, myself included, for the last time. I remember the feeling of regret that stayed with me afterwards, the wonder at what might have been, but also the pride in our – possibly naïve, but nevertheless well-intentioned – attempts to make things better for footballers in the college.

Ten years later – on St Patrick's Day 2013 – I watched with tears in my eyes as a man who played with me for three years on Trinity teams won Man of the Match as his club became the first ever side from Roscommon to win the All-Ireland Senior Club Championship.

Karol Mannion played a huge role in helping his team recover from an eight-point deficit that day to win the match. Real leadership stuff. Doing it in adversity, when it mattered most.

I contacted him to congratulate him. I was proud to know him, proud to have played with him and delighted that he had helped a Connacht club to glory on the biggest stage. When I knew him in Trinity, he didn't strike you as a footballer who would have a performance like that in him some day. But I saw the improvement happening up close, firstly in Trinity, then in Sligo vs Roscommon games.

I don't know what kind of a college football experience I would have had if I went to UCD. Or IT Sligo. Or Queens. I may have seen friends and colleagues win All-Stars, or multiple All-Irelands, instead of All-Ireland club titles. I may have won more matches, or I may not have even played. I may never have gained the experience of helping to make and see through big decisions, or I might have learned more from seeing how a winning culture works. I'll never know, but I certainly wouldn't swap any of them for the college football experience I had.

In Trinity, we were fighting against the odds from day one. I don't know what things are like for GAA players there now. Part of me hopes that facilities have improved, but the other part doesn't, because I think that what we went through brought us closer. Made us more determined. And, honestly, it made a bunch of white males from middle-class backgrounds know what it was like to feel downtrodden, if only for a while, and in regard to something that in the bigger picture wasn't really that important.

But at the time it was. And that's the point. My Psychology and Philosophy degree didn't take up too many hours in the day, and, if I'm honest, my interest in studying hard was not huge. So when I look back at Trinity days they are defined by football. With the lads in college, but also with my club and county back home. And for someone who was away in boarding school and then out of the country for seven consecutive years, this was invaluable. Making new friends, reconnecting with old ones, becoming part of a community once again, feeling grounded. Hugely important stuff.

So while it really wasn't set up for us to succeed, and our on-field endeavours certainly came up short of what we would have hoped, maybe we were just too young to know that success can come in many different forms.

Kieran Quinn (TCD 1999–2003; Psychology and Philosophy) is a pianist, composer, producer, writer and teacher from Sligo. He has released four albums and an EP since 2013, and his renowned Theme Nights are the hottest tickets in Sligo each year. He also packed out Dublin's Vicar Street in 2019. He is a leader in youth musical education in his native county. He presents the music podcast 'In The Lamplight' and is a regular blogger at www.kieranquinn.ie. Kieran also played Gaelic Football for Coolera-Strandhill and Sligo, and was part of the 2007 Sligo team that won the third Connacht Championship in the county's history.

SLIPPING THROUGH

cliona loughnane

NOW WITH laptop-phones in our pockets it seems a historical joke, but in our first year you got your exam results via large cabinet boards hung at the Nassau Street entrance. Academic ratings strung up for all to see, a black and white score with your end-of-year order of merit. I was away when the rolls of paper were unfurled, the glass-fronted wooden frame opened and the results hung up. My father – he who tore my essays to shreds at odd hours of the night, always just before submission deadline – said he'd go in and check. Called me. 'How have I done?' I asked. I really wasn't sure, hard to tell in your first year. Maybe it was better than I thought. He talked me down to where I was, midway on the board. 'A 63 in both' – long pause – 'At least you're consistent.'

By which he meant not good. You're not good.

Those wooden boards at Nassau Street have since been replaced by six flat TV screens advertising the university's attractions. The Trinity College I went to in 2000 is a particular Trinity. A Trinity in a time and place, with a distinct Dublin outside the walls and a particular me inside. My unholy trinity.

Ireland then was in a spike of change – character-limited string texts started to buzz, the Provisionals were decommissioning, Gay Byrne had started making millionaires™ on RTÉ, farmers were walking cows across disinfected carpets to stop the spread of foot and mouth, homes were being renovated into boom houses, parents buying second cars and real, squeezed orange juice. There was New World wine. There were credit cards. The organized numismatic carried two wallets to separate euros and punts, and when phone credit ran out we sent 'Call Me' missives. The government claimed 400 new jobs a day.

Trinity held its own, resolute. Moneyed for centuries, it seemed unchallenged by the boom, or inevitable bust.

I was where my family had been for most my life – a rented Victorian terrace where the landlord came monthly to cut the grass and have mum make him dinner. Mum tried for security for us, but the display and reality never reconciled. Like the landlord's cream curtains in the sitting room which were both prickly and grimy to the touch. You can mostly live with someone else's curtains. One day, years in, she covered them with sheer green chiffon. The chiffon pinned on top of the heavier material with miniature bulldog clips, the type used in offices to keep papers together. Pulled back and forth each day, the chiffon slipped and gathered strangely, swinging symbols of impermanence. Now, I see I was looking for a home wherever I went. School wasn't it, just a place to put seven years down and not look back. Home-*home* was all pretending. Trinity might be the place.

...

You can do English and History most places. I chose Trinity because I could walk there. Forty minutes from the Finglas Road to College Green. I liked that it was close. And in my craven, adolescent heart I liked what it could signify – that I'd got more points. It meant something – Trinity – something that could build me up from the outside. So, out the blue front door I went in October, turn right, past car-clogged Hart's corner, into Phibsboro, sometimes past the monolithic shopping centre, sometimes down the Royal Canal by the chocolate-box library and Mountjoy Prison, through the Broadstone and towards a grimier, year-2000 O'Connell Street. Then, a straight line to Dublin University.

The way to enter Trinity – the Front Arch – off College Green is a little opening into a big space. Sometimes the smallness of the opening, the welcome, seems purposeful. A small, curved door, so tight people have to hold back and take their turn to pass – slipping through – around you, the heavy wooden and metal gate surrounded by a vast building of traffic-grimed granite and

Portland stone. Once inside and through the domed vestibule, space releases out. An open plot with green trees. It's a gap in the city enfolded by consistent buildings, an eye salve from the variances of the streets outside. Front Square breathed out solidity and I'd breathe in.

At the beginning, walking through the square I had a hesitancy making a claim on this part of the city. Many Dubliners, new to Trinity, will say, 'I didn't know you could walk in here; I didn't know you could just come in.' Because walking in Trinity is walking in a particular place, differentiated from Capel, Westmoreland, Pearse Streets. Teenagers in tweed, decades before Peaky Blinders democratized it, with that Trinity-shabby style belonging allows. 'This blazer? My Grandad's.' Club ties, full-cotton ancient rugby jerseys, holed cashmere cardigans, wrinkled silk shirts and a sailors' convention of brown, white-soled Dubarry shoes and twisted leather laces. And there's the sound landscape – a Trinity voice – or at least it was to me, because that's where I first really heard it, this disharmony of satisfied South Dublin. Which I critique because, after four years, it is my voice now. My Dublin–country mix duly reconstituted, tilting aspirationally upwards. This accent, which means I still sound like a thing I don't feel.

...

I was lucky to have one familiar face from day one. Mary and I weren't the first to come down from the school on Glasnevin Hill to the Arts Block; small numbers had traipsed down for years. But I still felt out of place. On College Green, standing inside the gates but before the curved wooden door, in the antechamber between Dublin city centre and Trinity's Front Square, I felt proud I went there. With teenage pomp, I even hoped people walking by noticed this was my place. But on College ground, walking towards the Lecky Library in that first year I was often scratchy with discomfort. Feeling suddenly too large *in* my body, desperately aware of where skin stops and the world begins, bumping up against it, instead of swimming through. I was awkward trying to grasp things, catching up with meanings.

Not so inept that I didn't make really good friends – twenty-years-on friends. But I was comparing me to everyone.

I thought they were much more certain. Most came from private schools, must have known more people here. Did it make it easier to feel in their rightful place? I don't know; it was never discussed. We present as blank slates to College. Which none of us are, teeming with the marking out of childhoods.

Like all of us, I was carrying a mix-up inside. And like Trinity, I didn't have a foundational father. I too had a Queen mother,[*] fixing and sorting to try and give my sister and I a clear path. My father extolled his working-class income but middle-class education. It really was next to no income, and Mum ran the family with her salary. We lived in our rented house. We were stretched, more than some, much, much less than others. But the pretence was tiring and pointless. Living the simple short story where we're a family like everyone else's in this North Dublin suburb. Pretending to be like my parents' college friends, to be more than afloat. But simultaneously say we're choosing an artistic life over security and sense. Say money doesn't matter, that we're 'better-off' that way. The effort made me attuned to the gaps between people's experiences. The long temporariness of renting meant that just before reaching two decades' tenure we were told to leave. A month before my final exams, Mum and I loaded the small bits of furniture that didn't come with the house into a borrowed trailer to move across the city. I couldn't be sure that the trajectory of life was upwards, onwards. My parents' position showed that.

Inside me were the deposits of my life – my school academics, my parents' degrees, and the certain trajectory of college for me – with adulthood, the withdrawals were only beginning to be felt. Trinity seemed to scrape away something in my epidermis, the loss of another layer of confidence. It injected outsider-ness, or it brought it to the surface. Though I think I hid it well by keeping my Trinity life simple and my relationship monogamous, and by avoiding the stretch of societies or student politics.

Other colleges get out their rituals – and gowns – for graduations, Trinity weaves them straight through term-time; Commons dining, members' clubs, debate black-tie as lecture-wear Wednesdays and Thursdays. All the archaic rules of Trinity – only wear black and white beneath your graduating gowns – that add up to privilege. Some students embrace *in toto*, others ignore, some laugh. I didn't know my own thought, one part wanting to reject but without

---

[*] Trinity College was founded in 1592 by Queen Elizabeth I as the 'Queen Mother' of a new university that was modelled after the collegiate universities of Oxford and Cambridge. https://en.wikipedia.org/wiki/Trinity_College_Dublin

that confident power. Later, green Mary Janes nudging out from beneath my graduation dress in a coward's rebellion. No matter what a father said, I'm not consistent.

...

Maybe now – almost forty – I'd question why the place had me so unnerved. What was it about other people that I wanted? Now, I might turn my troubles outward, but at eighteen, I burrowed inside, questioned why I didn't claim my space as others seemed able. Even those much less supported than I, up from the country, or first in the family to go to college. I didn't even deserve the not-fitting-in.

But I felt it and I feel it now – that sense of shame that I couldn't claim my place. I looked – soon I sounded – like a fitter-in. I couldn't decode my discomfort with Trinity, First Year Critical Theory classes of de Saussure and Lacan no help here, because I wanted it. I couldn't hold onto my fleeting awareness of 'it' as pompous. I wanted it. To walk in through Front Arch and feel I belonged, to walk through life and see success and self-satisfaction ahead.

On high alert for insult, cowed by what I perceived as the prestige of the place, my school days' confidence lurched down. I constrained myself defensively, which meant I found it hard to place all the commonalities between me and everyone else. I was too focused on picking up on things that maybe don't mean what you think they mean, don't exclude you in the way you imagine. And even if they do, who cares? Who's this smirking legal student to you, and why, the day after he kissed you – and you feel clear-headed remorse – does he have to be told walking across Fellow's Square that you got the points for Law too?

Primed for exclusion, I didn't have it in me to enlist in the Hist or the Phil. Too busy debating with myself. I didn't join my group of friends branching out into play production in the Samuel Beckett, kept my own dramas to Monday's cheap pints in the Buttery. I tried to do something, so once a week I'd leave campus proper to go to Pearse Street's Goldsmith Hall and volunteer with the Trinity Access Programmes, tutoring students from schools with a college progression rate far below my own. I remember them as a youthful cocktail of funny, alive and bored when they turned up. I was probably nervous and gushing. I was meant to make Trinity feel – as close as it physically was – a real possibility.

...

I've long felt humiliation that I didn't thrive and anger that I didn't question, didn't challenge, didn't make it marginally better for the next me to come to college. Sometimes there's something deep inside us that makes us feel not good enough, and sometimes the way the outside world is set up reflects that back to us and makes it worse.

Trinity, the place, exudes permanence, with geometric squares, repeating building styles, a grey calm. Trinity's community exudes generational success. Constancies I couldn't really relate to. My lack of assuredness felt Trinity-specific after I went on to other colleges. They seemed more mundane and claimable; there was more of a straight line from my school, home, my Dublin, to NUI campuses, casual with county colours. But I was four years, five, six older and Trinity had trained me in college working, so whether the comfort was made by years, or by the place, is hard to untangle.

In Trinity, I sought out small belongings. I liked the Buttery Bar. How past 6 pm there would be a bouncer, stopping non-Trinity-ites. So, we – my friends and I – all got in, except sometimes Mary, still seventeen and with the tell-tale underage stripe across her ID card. I liked the Arts Block, where I spent most of my time. It had the civic look of other buildings from the 1970s, although the old men of the college remained overseeing all, masculine names over each lecture hall. I found my group here, drinking our tea (just 10p for the hot water in Styrofoam cups, bags brought from home). My gentle group of college friends brought together by a coincidence of CAO and a love of reading, solidified in growing up together for those four years. On the upper floors of the Arts Block, over the Jonathan Swift Theatre, the Edmund Burke Hall, I liked how the proportions shifted to school-familiar concrete-brick corridors. Office pods – one the School of English – curved off the straight, strip-lit corridors. Nicely scratchy carpets at this level, tough but encouraging you to sit waiting for tutorials. There was a particular smell throughout the Block – dry and concretey – perhaps the burning of dust on metal radiators, a municipal aroma that brought me back to the Dublin City public libraries where so much good time was spent – the long, promising shelves of the Ilac, the children's room in Ballymun. Three buildings sharing an aesthetic of slightly blown glass, internal pebble-dashed concrete, large vibrant textured canvases, public art for public buildings. And Trinity is itself a public place, land granted by the Dublin Corporation in the sixteenth century.

But even the more homely Arts Block was really a Brutalist bunker, turning away from the city and in on the controlled internal squares. On ground level there is no sight out to Nassau Street, and on the upper floors most windows are small apertures off long corridors. They are slits, like the fortress openings we learned about from medievalist Professor Robinson, set at a just-so angle that you have to twist your head to spy onto Dawson Street. Trinity sometimes felt it was holding you in.

...

Please don't let me mislead. Mine was not a student penury. How little I was disadvantaged. I was being supported to keep up. I didn't have to fight to be allowed to go, to defer four years of work. While my parents slipped below the lives and salary expected of their starts, Mum managed it again, relatives were generous. Mine was a leisured undergrad.

I see my Trinity years' discomfort as about confidence, my lack. But it was also about class.

Class is a stupid thing. I renounce it nowadays, would have liked if I could have overruled my constant attention to it then. But in Trinity I lived on high alert for status, because of an inbuilt snobbery of my own, honed by ritual and survival, attuned to the signals of the middle class – 'the half-talk code of mysteries and the wink-and-elbow language of delight'* – born in a family life full of fantasizing. Trinity knocked against the pretence; I was fully exposed now in a playground of the privately educated, the widely travelled, the extra-curriculared.

Still, reject class and it'll still be everywhere, full of consequences and very real: solidified in salaries, in homes, in belonging and in power. Checked-up on, adjudicated, scented on our clothes, bread-crumbed in our accents, clear to see because we all know the tells. But, never talked about. We're 'The Emergency' people without a post-war settlement. We're Fianna Fáil, we're Fine Gael, we're Labour. We're Northsiders, we're D4. We're dairy farmers, we're townies.

---

* Patrick Kavanagh, 'Inniskeen Road: July Evening'. https://www.tcd.ie/English/patrickkavanagh/inniskeenroad
.html

When it comes to class in Ireland – especially in 2000 when a boom is booming and raising all boats, allegedly – 'whatever you say, say nothing'.*

What has happened in the time since I first walked into Trinity a Junior Freshman in a new millennium? Ireland went up and crashed down. But the strata largely stayed the same – boom-time SSIA savings on second properties, raising rents on short-term contracts. The Trinity of my mind, and the one I walk through sometimes as a shortcut twenty years on, still feels like a small enclosure for a privileged few. Even today, the better-off dominate; Trinity has amongst the lowest number of students with grants. And outside, the architecture of 2020 grows up higher than ever before in twenty-floor office blocks and glazed hotel groups , quick and shiny, while Front Square sturdily stands.

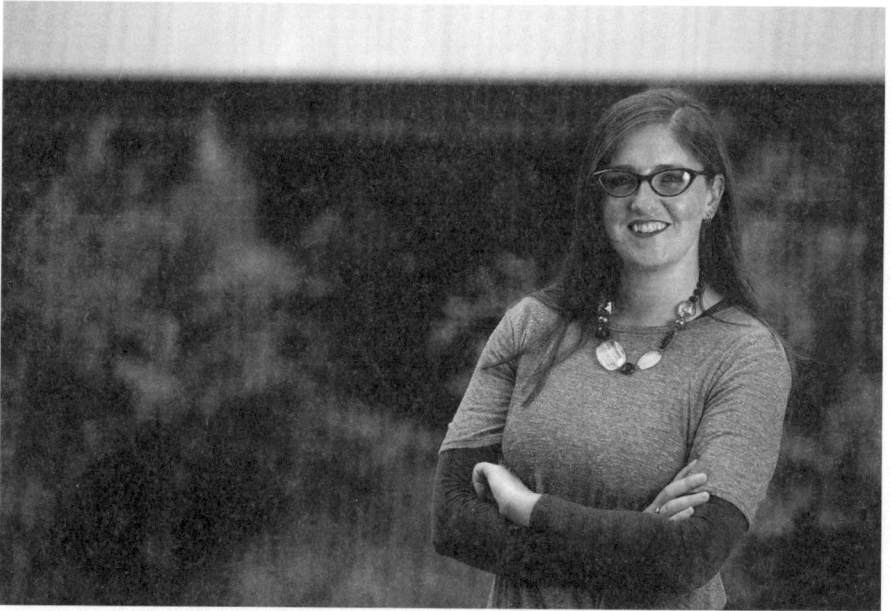

After Trinity, **Dr Cliona Loughnane** (TCD 2000–4; English Literature and History) studied social science and worked for more than a decade in advocacy and policy roles in health and women's rights organizations. She is currently a post-doctoral researcher on a project re-imagining care provision in Ireland following the pandemic.

---

* Seamus Heaney (1975). 'Whatever You Say, Say Nothing'. *North*. Faber and Faber.

'AND SO YOU SHALL'

annie colleran

I **FIRST** set eyes on Trinity at the age of fourteen on my first ever trip to Dublin. I had spent most of my life until that point in Adelaide, Australia. That summer my brother Thom and I had been dispatched to our grandmother in Fermoy, Co. Cork, to water our Irish roots, reconnect with family and broaden our worldview. Grandma kept us busy with an itinerary of social calls to our extended family interspersed with cultural outings. We pretty much did everything she did – Active Retirement history tours, holy hours of obligation, dances and lots of mass. One such outing was a day trip to Dublin. We took the bus up from Fermoy to the capital and then took a double-decker bus tour of the city sights. Our tour guide was a salt-of-the-earth Dub, and I was riveted both to what he said and to the amazing, unexpected way that he said it. As the bus rounded the curve of College Green and Trinity came into view, I strained to see the tantalizing glimpse of student life visible through Front Arch and remarked to Grandma that I would love to study there. Grandma replied without a moment's pause, 'And so you shall.' And that was it, with the grand-matriarchal permission sought and granted, the die was cast.

My plan to study in Trinity remained intact while my family moved to Belgium and then two years later back to Australia. I enrolled in a school in the Brisbane suburb of Ashgrove. I stuck a picture of the Campanile into my school journal and referred to it when my peers queried my post-school plans. In our peaceful – verging on insular – suburb, I might as well have said I was planning to attend college on the moon. My parents, in their usual spirit of adventure and with their signature non-directive parenting style, did not make any attempt to quell my romantic notion of studying in Trinity. My mother, as a London Irish émigré in Australia, was delighted at the prospect of me returning to my cultural and spiritual home, albeit one of which I knew little. My summer visits had given me some cultural grounding. I had learned of *Blackboard Jungle*, the *Late Late Show*, the RTÉ Guide, the Eurovision. Other than that, I was really stepping out into the unknown and, as it turned out, leaving home forever.

However, untroubled by any second thoughts, I had an eighteenth birthday party which doubled as a send-off and headed off. There would be no popping home for a few days, there would be no Christmas at home for the foreseeable future. It was a fairly drastic move, made unblinkingly with the naïve confidence of a teenager. Travelling from the opposite hemisphere, I was six months out of sync with the Irish school and college year. My gap half-year was spent working as an au pair, and, when this experience was not to my liking, I moved in with Grandma. There followed more rounds of visiting and more cultural integration, including attending the CBC Mitchelstown debs and Saturday nights out in the Mitchelstown hotspot, The Clon, with my cousins. Finally, one happy day, the postman brought an offer of a place in Trinity for my first-choice course, European Studies. Things continued to go my way when I got a much-coveted place in Trinity Hall. The stage was set for my Trinity Tale to begin.

Trinity Hall was all that I had hoped it would be. It was akin to a particularly raucous boarding school, but with no hall monitors and a lot more alcohol. Living in such close proximity with fellow students meant that within a week we felt that we had always known each other. The ensemble cast included a beleaguered live-in warden who spent his time admonishing bold students, sent to him for punishment by the two pantomime-villain dames who ran the office. There was a team of generally benevolent bumbling security guards and a squad of 'skips', older Dublin ladies who cleaned the residence while tutting about the state of the place and questioning how the young people were raised. The residents, of which there were fewer than 200 in total, were a mix of mostly sensible Europeans and a younger, giddier contingent of Irish students, away from home for the first time, liberated from the intense and stultifying Leaving Cert cycle and ready to have the craic. It was with this second group that I most identified.

The set-up in Halls at the time consisted of shared and single bedrooms, shared kitchens and two large social spaces – a television room and the common room. I didn't spend much time in the television room. It was usually reasonably full and yet horribly quiet, with any talking met with aggressive shushing. Screenings of *Friends* were a pseudo-religious experience, with packed pews and reverential silence interspersed with loud guffawing as the plotlines dictated. The common room, on the other hand, was a rolling relay of a house party.

The common room was the place to gather, share bottles of cheap vodka, nasty wine and even nastier cider. If you were not sure about the wisdom of yet another night out, and were thinking about potentially having an early night in, a stroll through the common room would disabuse you of this notion. You would realize that an epic night was kicking off, that everyone was going out and that if you didn't, death by FOMO might arise. The term FOMO (Fear of Missing Out) had not yet been coined, and yet the feeling was very much real.

It was in this hedonistic bubble that I met my soulmate, future husband and father to my five children. I often wonder at the fact that the boyfriend I chose then as a nineteen-year-old, heedless Fresher still suits me now as a fairly socially responsible 41-year-old. It is probably because what I liked about him then, I still do now: his ability to strike up and hold a conversation with anybody – regardless of race, creed, age or gender – his boundless energy, his spontaneity, his infectious good humour. He asked me to type a constitutional law essay for him, as he had left it too late to get it typed by the Students' Union typing service. How quaint it seems today, the notion of handwriting an essay, submitting it to a typing pool, having no laptop and no IT skills, and yet this was the *process du jour* and indeed *deus ex machina* that brought us together.

With a pace akin to a cheesy Disney movie, the protagonist (me) and the love interest (JH) moved from cordial, nodding acquaintance to full-blown, besotted devotion. We socialized in the rolling maul of Halls nights out and in between hung out constantly, disrupted by the requirement to attend classes from time to time. The year sped towards its conclusion, there were impromptu picnics in the lush grass of Halls and St Stephen's Green, there was the Trinity Ball, there were exams and then there was the summer. My family had moved to Galway during the course of my first year and, as luck would have it, were living within five minutes of his family. Summer involved working during the day and hanging out every evening. We were as carefree as we would ever be, because before the autumn rolled around, our extended kidulthood was over and I was pregnant.

My second year in Trinity could not have been more different to my first. I went back to college with an imperceptible bump. I had told some close friends about the pregnancy, which proved to be a mistake as this news travelled quickly and extensively through the college grapevine. It was strange and uncomfortable to become a subject of gossip, of scandal and of widespread speculation. I felt that I was being looked at, whispered about, discussed. As my bump became more noticeable, I became a walking bill-board for what happens if you're not careful. It is only when you begin to feel different that you become aware of just how homogenous the student body is. It was an isolating experience. I fell out with my main group of friends. I discovered that my wider group of friends were largely drinking buddies, a category of friend I clearly had no use for at this point. I took this opportunity to apply myself slightly harder to my studies and stayed in college until the week our baby was due, despite not being able to tuck myself into the stingily proportioned desk seats in the Ed Burke lecture theatre. I had our daughter during the Patrick's Day break after Hilary Term and returned to college after the two-week break, leaving our tiny girl in the experienced hands of my mother while I got through the six weeks of Trinity Term and the Second Year exams.

Third Year came. I returned to Trinity after the summer with our six-month-old baby girl in tow. I got a place for her in the Trinity on-campus crèche and secured accommodation nearby thanks to the help of the then Students' Union Welfare Officer. I had been due to go on Erasmus for Third Year. It is a compulsory component of the European Studies course, but I received a reprieve from this as I really couldn't fathom moving abroad with a baby and breaking up our little family of three. From being in a small class of thirty-five European Studies students, I went to being a class of one, though I was joined by a second classmate who hated her time in Paris and was allowed to return home and complete the year in Trinity. We shared our lectures, as before, with BESS, History, Politics and language students.

I figured out life as a student parent – maximizing my time while she was in the crèche, having cosy nights in, rambling days wandering round the city and negotiating alternate nights out with her papa. My circle had shrunk considerably, and now that I no longer could party as my main hobby I felt I needed to make new friends and have more purpose and direction in my life. I decided to join the Students' Union, initially as a class rep for my class of two, and then the next year I joined the Executive Committee as Women's Officer.

Having benefitted from the support and advice of the Welfare Officer, it seemed like a logical step to run for election for the position during Fourth Year.

Final Year was great in many ways. I felt that academically something clicked for me, and I knew how to research, structure and write an essay without much sweat. Our thoughts turned to life after college. I applied for lots of steady, sensible jobs in the 'milk round' as a safety net, but my sights were set on the Students' Union. I had a campaign team made up of pals from Halls and Law students roped in by my boyfriend and campaign manager. Running for Students' Union election is a proxy for the real thing. It was a three-week whirlwind of putting up posters, handing out manifestos, making lecture addresses, speaking at hustings, meeting, greeting, culminating in a high-drama count night.

I was duly elected, and so, after the small matter of finishing my final year, I moved in with my baby girl to cosy, ramshackle rooms in Front Square. Front Square was her garden, and the city was her playground. She often attended protests and always attended executive meetings, doodling quietly on flip-charts with highlighters as animated discussions and heated debates took place. I enjoyed my time in House 6, the Students' Union Headquarters. The role of Welfare Officer suited me. My days were a busy mix of organizing health campaigns, representing students' views and interests on college committees and also meeting with individual students to provide advice and support. It was a lot of responsibility, but I appreciated the autonomy and the opportunity to be involved in the fabric of the college, part of the decision-making bodies and part of the great tradition of TCDSU leaders and change-makers. Trinity is a village within the city, and I was a very entrenched villager. At one point I realized that I hadn't stepped off campus for nearly two weeks and really hadn't missed the outside world!

Annie Colleran with John Hugh and daughter Aoife Colleran.

My year as Welfare Officer was in full swing when the College calendar moved on to SU election time again. I felt that I still had unfinished business with student politics and threw my hat into the ring for SU President. I was delighted to get elected for a second sabbatical term and this time to have a broader remit and arguably even more responsibility. My sabbatical team included two girls who would become my closest college friends, and we worked hard but also had a lot of fun doing it. We ran the Union by consensus and through a common desire to do our best for our students. I find it hard to recount this period without sounding sentimental or like a LinkedIn profile. But these two extra Trinity years in my Tale cemented both my love for the college and the education it offered me. Over the years, I have drawn on the memory bank of experiences to galvanize me for new challenges. There is little that I have faced in the intervening years that is more daunting than fielding hostile questions at hustings, addressing several thousand students on a rally or even voicing dissent at College board meetings.

The year went all too quickly, and before I knew it I was shopping for suits and readying myself for the corporate world. After living on-campus for two years, the thought of living any distance from town was an anathema to us, so we moved to Temple Bar and walked to work and school through campus on a daily basis. It was, and still is, a touchstone for me, a place to go to step away from life for a few minutes, revisit old memories and escape from new pressures.

Nine years ago, my college sweetheart and I formalized our relationship by marrying in the college chapel. And now, through a combination of happenstance and years of strong hinting, our firstborn, our college baby, has returned to Trinity, to her playground, to study medicine. And so my Trinity Tale continues vicariously, and I can content myself with hearing about what has changed and what, thankfully, remains the same.

After leaving Trinity, **Annie Colleran** (née Gatling; TCD 1998–2002; European Studies) joined Bank of Ireland's graduate programme. She worked in various roles in the bank, including HR, change, retail banking and business banking, before taking an extended career break in 2014 to spend more time with her family. She is currently channelling her energies into voluntary roles, being Treasurer of a parents' association, sitting on a school board and coaching youth GAA. She lives in Dundrum with her husband and five children.

A YEAR IN A THOUSAND

sarah benson

MY POSTGRADUATE YEAR in Trinity College straddled the 'millennium year': 1999 into 2000. 2000 was a year when the world breathed a sigh of relief, having been braced for the apocalypse that the 'millennium bug' was to bring: destroying all computer data in a single nanosecond as the clock struck midnight. Microwaves would revolt. Flights would tumble from the skies. None of which happened, of course.

I'm recalling this now, sat in a diner on 5th Avenue in Manhattan drinking coffee on Friday, 13 March 2020, and hoping that this evening my flight will leave JFK unimpeded and ferry me back to my home and family. This, before governments invoke yet more extreme measures of containment to suppress infections as the world grapples with the rapidly spreading, novel COVID-19 virus. A different bug and a new prospective apocalypse. Two decades on, but still strange days.

Of course, at twenty-four years old the prospective End of Days did not put much of a dent in my lifestyle as a Trinity student. I was working part-time in a bar and restaurant and generally enjoying being young. I wonder, though, if that is the same for twenty-somethings today? After all, far from the return to the Stone Age anticipated on the eve of midnight 1999, we are now utterly tech saturated – verging on an information overload that keeps us all so plugged in, so aware and so anxious.

That is something that strikes me forcibly when I compare the 'then and now'. At that time in Trinity, we just about had working email, and the internet as an effective academic research tool was barely a fully formed concept. It was clunky, slow and inaccessible, and came with a 'dial-up' noise so irritatingly wailing that it kept me scuttling back to old-fashioned paper sources rather than endure it. It was also a serious linguistic challenge then to try to guess the magic combination of words that early iterations of search engines required in order to source anything even vaguely useful. In 2000, a company called 'Google' was really up and coming, vying for attention along with Netscape Navigator's several search engine offerings, which included Yahoo among others; the results were still a million miles from the instant and precise results we receive today. Also, it's true to say that I have never and will never be accused of being an 'early adopter' of any kind of technical innovation.

Books and actual paper articles were therefore still very much a vital resource for the pursuit of academia. Having come from UCD, where I did my BA and where access to the library and withdrawal of books is available to all undergraduates, I realized quite quickly how lucky I was as a Trinity postgrad. I was permitted to withdraw – and keep for weeks at a time – up to eight books or papers, while the poor undergrads could only read inside the library buildings those books which the greedy postgrads had not already snagged. This felt rather unfair to me, but, as the beneficiary of the arrangement, I confess that I did not raise any complaint. It was a phenomenal discovery to me that Trinity had a copyright library. For the uninitiated, this means that it receives and retains a copy of every single publication made in Ireland and the UK. There are over five million publications available. Often these had to be ordered by submitted request from the mysterious-sounding 'stacks'. I had visions of teetering piles of paper, stacked to the ceiling, row upon row and as far as the eye could see, in some ancient and cavernous building.

I was studying for an MPhil in Gender and Women's Studies, having tracked in this direction through a combination of an elected Critical Theory module I took for my Bachelors in English and where I started reading feminist theories, among others, and also through meeting and having some incredibly enlightening conversations with an older feminist activist while volunteering with the student helpline Niteline. At that time, Niteline served the students of UCD and Trinity, later expanding to cover students at additional universities.

This meant that after graduating from UCD and moving to Trinity I could continue to volunteer with Niteline. During my final year and postgraduate year, myself and a colleague also coordinated the recruitment and training for all new volunteers. The training delivery, regular team meetings and service delivery itself all took place on the Trinity campus in a range of different buildings, but no one other than ourselves and the Students' Union representatives who facilitated our access knew where.

At that time, anyone involved in this service was sworn to secrecy about it. It was important not to inhibit any student from feeling they could reach out and speak to someone completely anonymously, and in confidence. It was decided that students shouldn't know who among their peers might be on the end of that line. This also protected our boundaries as volunteers from a relatively small population. It was years after I finished before I publicly divulged my involvement with Niteline.

A consequence of secrecy was a very close-knit, mutually supportive group based on our shared work and experience. Every week we listened to the loneliness, pain, confusion, anxiety, hurts and fears that some of our fellow students were suffering. They reached out late in the night for comfort, reassurance, information and support. I remember the young woman who was having suicidal thoughts after a rape she had not disclosed to anyone else; the international student who was feeling completely alone and struggling with cultural differences – wanting nothing more than to find ways to help him make new friends. I remember the terrible pressure people were piling on themselves at exam time, the crippling fear of failure; the students who were struggling with their sexuality; and so much more. My volunteering gave me such privileged insights into my peers' experiences and a lifelong appreciation for not taking things at face value where people's well-being is concerned.

As a helpline team, we shared together the ups (such as the boozy bonding weekends away, building great friendships) and the downs (the memorable sofa that was donated for our helpline room and which may or may not have given most of us scabies) of Niteline. From my involvement in Niteline between 1996 and 2001, we were also subject to a relatively minor but nonetheless notable challenge in our service delivery, which really speaks to the times we were living in – and how far Irish society has now come. In 1992, with the Fourteenth Amendment to the Irish constitution, the legal restrictions on sharing information about abortion services available in other jurisdictions (of course, there were none in Ireland at the time) were lifted. The 'conditions for provision of this information' were then legislated for in the Regulation of Information (Services Outside the State for Termination of Pregnancies) Act, 1995. However, prior to December 1992, it had been a crime to even give women the phone number of an abortion clinic in Liverpool or elsewhere.

In 1991, the Union of Students in Ireland, and the UCD and TCD Students' Unions (along with named individuals including the president of the TCD Students' Union, Ivana Bacik, and others from TCDSU), had been accused of sharing this information in student guidebooks, and a landmark court case ensued: *SPUC* v. *Grogan and Others*. This resulted in a permanent court injunction to prevent any of the accused parties (including, by association, the student service Niteline) from sharing abortion information with students, which persisted even after the constitutional change until the case finally concluded in 1997.

The USI and individual parties were defended by one Mary Robinson, and (as one then defendant explained to me) they 'won, but lost on a technicality'. The case extended to both the European Court of Justice and the Irish Supreme Court and could have (but happily did not) bankrupted the Students' Unions involved, and jailed individually named defendants.

This injunction lifted in 1997, and up to that point Niteline had been in frequent receipt of vexatious efforts to entrap members giving 'illegal' information through fake reports of crisis pregnancy by anti-choice callers seeking 'advice'. Even after the injunction lifted, that did not deter these groups from trying to catch Niteline out as breaching the still specific and narrow parameters of the 1995 Act. Therefore, all new volunteers during this period had to be briefed to be vigilant to the 'undercover and recorded calls' (a few of which I took myself), mounted by the likes of Youth Defense and SPUC – anti-choice groups with significant on-campus activity at this time. These calls were invariably from men, who would disclose that their girlfriend had become pregnant and that they didn't want a baby, and would then proceed to try and lure us into giving specific and very detailed referral information to abortion service providers, which if we had would have no doubt led to further mischievous legal action of some kind against the student services.

The battle on campuses to achieve women's reproductive rights really was such at this time. On the incredibly emotional day of 25 May 2018 – the day when we finally repealed the Eighth Amendment to the Irish constitution, making abortion services legal in Ireland – I recalled the dangerous absurdity of these experiences. One friend involved in running a pro-choice Freshers' Week information stand in UCD was actually physically attacked by their neighbour on a pro-life/anti-choice stand, who took their zealous mission to 'defend the unborn' extremely literally.

Of course, Niteline was just one aspect of my campus experience, but it was an important one, which was hugely instrumental in guiding me in my career path. I continued to develop training and facilitation skills, which I employed in my first role in the community and voluntary sector as Training Co-Coordinator with the Blanchardstown Traveller Community Development Project, and in every role I've held since. The experience was also fundamental to my subsequent role as Manager of the National Domestic Violence Helpline.

The Masters course itself then gave me the foundations I needed to give full expression to my inherent feminist values and principles, and awakened in me a burning desire to pursue gender equality and, especially, to end violence against women and girls. Twenty years on, and currently heading up Women's Aid, a national domestic violence organization – having for the nine years prior been CEO to an agency supporting victims of commercial sexual exploitation, including victims of sex trafficking – I look to the progress we can mark in eradicating gender inequality and gender-based violence, but also see the backlash that sometimes feels like we are moving two steps forwards and one step back.

I completed my thesis on the subject of 'cultural subjectivity' and the social construction of the female gender using article 41.2 of the Irish constitution as a case study. This is commonly known as the 'women in the home' article. Today, as I write, a citizen's assembly on gender equality has been convened, and it will focus as part of its terms of reference on this article. Perhaps it's not too much to hope that we may be close to the removal of this egregious article, to be replaced with a gender-neutral affirmation of the value of care work to society. So: forward momentum. However, at the same time, I return to my earlier reflections on technology, and I'm reminded of a particular experience from my time at Trinity that, when compared to today, exemplifies a concurrent step backwards.

One of my course colleagues (who remains a friend today and who works now as a state prosecutor in New York, with a particular remit to prosecute child exploitation and domestic violence offences) was conducting her thesis on correlations between domestic violence and pornography.

As part of her field research, she was granted access to consult with residents of a refuge and participants in a domestic-violence perpetrator programme. At the same time, she needed to research the prevalence and content of pornography. In Dublin at that time, general access to this was pretty much limited to a few shady sex shops around the Capel Street area, and my friend duly trawled through these. But she felt the shop owners were not forthcoming and she was being inhibited in her objective to undertake a comparative analysis of the range of pornography available: from 'soft' to 'hardcore' scenarios.

Therefore, in the spirit of academic endeavour, the two of us embarked on a part-holiday/part-research assignment to Amsterdam. We balanced our days between the canals and museums and immersion in the red-light district, where shop owners were far more forthcoming than their Irish counterparts about the breadth and range of hardcore, violent porn that was freely available.

This was an experience that cemented my gut instincts that porn is in no way designed or intended to ever satisfy women's sexual desires but is both inherently and explicitly misogynistic. Years later, work I did to support women who had been prostituted in the porn trade only affirmed this view.

What is most jarring, though, as I look back on that excursion, is the fact that in 2000 I had to get on a plane and fly to a niche neighbourhood of another country to access what is now potentially available on every twelve-year-old child's mobile phone – for free, and in violent and degrading forms that surpass even the worst that the vendors in the Reeperbahn tried to shock us with. This is notably concerning to me, being a mother to a twelve-year-old and a fourteen-year-old. So: two steps forward but …

On our return from Amsterdam and after so many hours trawling through grubby shops with distinctly slimy owners, the Trinity campus felt like an oasis of calm. It was contrastingly quaint and fanciful, being that time of the year when cricket was being played on the sports grounds, when you could sit in the sun on the grass with a drink from the 'Pav' and imagine you were occupying a completely different and insulated time.

I had really enjoyed my time in UCD, but the sprawling modern campus (excepting the peripheral buildings of Merville and Roebuck) was not an environment renowned for its architecture (so many iterations of concrete) or its centrality, perched as it is out on the N11 at Belfield. Trinity, on the other hand, has a beautiful, characterful campus combining charmingly ramshackle buildings and stately architecture like the famous Campanile (the belltower in Library Square which stands on the foundations of the original All Hallows monastery on which the college was built) and some great sculpture, including a Henry Moore. Students were accommodated in buildings with whimsical names like 'Botany Bay', and a place referred to as 'New Square' is actually 200 years old. The campus is also right in the heart of the city, which gives one the feeling, as a student, of being a part of something precious and privileged, while at the same time practical and amenable with our easy access to everything Dublin city centre has to offer.

My postgraduate class was small and quite international, with students from the United States, the UK and Turkey. Therefore, there was an element of the 'tourist' experience interwoven in our group's shared activities, both as students and friends. One such activity, arranged by the MPhil course coordinators, was a dinner at 'High Table' in the beautiful, wood-panelled dining hall, which we all dressed up for and attended the week after my aforementioned 'research trip' to Amsterdam. This was a rather unexceptional but tasty three-course meal served efficiently and with a high degree of ceremony, involving formally berobed scholars and an opening Latin grace. My American colleagues particularly enjoyed this experience, whereas the Irish among us preferred our informal post-prandial in the Buttery downstairs afterwards.

When we all reunited in our own robes the following year, however, I really was swept up in the ceremony of graduation and the sense of history and solemn achievement in ways I hadn't experienced for my undergraduate degree. I do think the physical environment of Trinity added a distinct level of gravitas. It's hard not to feel that sense of exclusive privilege being a part of this institution and it is very alluring, but as an alumnus now I donate specifically to the access programmes which support people from areas with low progression rates to higher education, helping them to reach their full educational potential, because it is so important that this 'exclusivity' is actually accessible to any bright mind who wants to study in Trinity College Dublin, no matter their background.

Reflecting back now, it's evident to me that Trinity in 1999–2000 was a catalytic year for me. In such a short period I absorbed so many diverse and contrasting experiences: imbued with ancient tradition, pomp and stiff ceremony; tantalizing access to the boundless knowledge of a copyright library; raw humanity of the quiet pain of students struggling to find themselves in the world; the shared power and resilience of mutually supportive peers. And, finally, there was my irrevocable awakening through my studies themselves to the hill women and girls still have to climb to gain equality, and essentially the lighting of the fire, passion and optimism to be a part of this movement. These abiding memories and lessons seem at once distant and wholly present as they have interwoven themselves into my personal and career development ever since.

Sarah Benson (TCD 1999–2000; MPhil Gender and Women's Studies) is the Chief Executive Officer of Women's Aid, Ireland. Throughout her career Sarah's passion for human rights, social justice and equality – in particular for women and girls – remains a constant feature. Sarah currently lives in Co. Dublin with her husband, son, daughter and cat.

ON AND OFF THE STAGE

erica murray

'SHE LOVES DRAMA' is a common phrase used to explain how someone craves attention and likes to socially stir the pot. 'She loves drama.' The same phrase used by my parents in a worrying tone when asked what their daughter was putting down on her CAO form.

My family are not theatre folk; they did not know what 'drama and theatre' was, let alone that you could study it. But still, in the way that their parents could never let them, they gave me a choice and an opportunity to follow my dreams. Drama it was.

Bearing in mind, I had seen two plays in my entire life, not including the ones I had been in or clips on YouTube of musicals … But something steadfast inside, I guess, told me it was for me. Maybe because I thought about it all the time. I wrote diaries about ideas and dialogue. I really tried to enjoy reading Shakespeare. I was obsessed with the idea of the theatre. I couldn't wait to fully immerse myself. So, imagine my surprise when on the first day of university I am told there are eight contact hours. Eight? But that's only one day spread across a week. What would I do in the evening?

During Freshers' Week, the Front Square of Trinity was covered in what seemed like thousands of stalls for different societies. I wandered around aimlessly, just glad to have something to fill the worrying amount of time on my hands. A girl who was standing in the queue for the library tour kindly asked me what I was studying. When I told her I was in drama, she grabbed my arm and looked deep into my eyes. 'You MUST join Players,' she said with such alarming intensity it sounded more like a threat than a piece of advice. I thought I'd better take her seriously, and I sought out this 'Players' stall which turned out to be the slang name for the DU Players drama society, and nothing to do with sport or dating multiple people at once.

At the society's stand there was a crowd of alarmingly loud people all wearing the same t-shirt, but each with their own personal twist, that said across it 'Come and Play'. After I wrote my name on a list, a 'goodie bag' was thrust into my arms filled with flyers for various auditions and about seventeen condoms. Was I supposed to use these? Was everyone else getting through them at that rate?

I was new to Dublin and knew absolutely no one. I had only been up to Dublin on day trips before now, so I didn't know the nice places to seek out or cosy spots to hide in. I spent lots of time wandering around the few streets I knew already. It seemed like no one had remembered to tell me about this part of moving away from home – that it was hard and very lonely. I felt completely lost at sea. So far, the practice of making up my own schedule had mostly consisted of studying alone in my bedroom, safe in the knowledge my family were all in the house. Even if I didn't see them, there was noise or conversation if I wanted it. Here, there was none. I had to start the painful process of making it up myself from scratch.

Those first days were so long. The reading for my course was not coming thick and fast, so instead I had the genius plan of reading whatever novel I was on at the time in the library. I would keep the book spread flat on the desk to hide the cover, lay an A4 pad right beside it and would jot down a random note every so often to really look the part. As if anyone was taking any notice. This elaborate ruse was found out when a classmate spotted me and asked me what I was reading for. They were worried they might have missed something. I had to admit it was just my book. They looked at me funny and made an excuse to leave. I was relieved.

Theatrics like this continued until the Thursday of the first week when I gave up and went home. I had been there for four long days. I couldn't hack 'the sesh' anymore. And by 'the sesh' I'm referring to being in my pyjamas at 6 pm, because I literally did not know what else to do, willing the day to be over.

For a girl who was ready to leave home from the age of fourteen, I was shocked at how homesick I felt. This wasn't what I had envisioned. I remember feeling incredibly jealous of the Dublin crew, mainly because they were already a crew, and they all seemed to know each other and have cosy red-brick houses in suburbs beginning with R to go home to in the evening.

I started at Trinity in 2009, just as the crash happened. The economy was crumbling, people were losing their jobs and homes, and I knew I was unbelievably lucky to be there and to have parents who were still supporting me on this dream, even though there was no guarantee of a steady income after it. And I hated it, every second of it. I thought the people were weird. I thought the course was strange. Actually, I didn't understand the course. It wasn't 'drama' as I had seen on YouTube.

Our first lecture was something called 'Semiotics'. I had no idea what this meant, and when I learned its meaning (the study of signs and symbols and their interpretation on stage) I had no idea why we were studying it. This was followed by a half-hearted essay on the subject, and I still have no idea why I got 62. I doubt it was ever read by anyone. I barely read it myself. I wrote it in a panic, submitted it (in those days you deposited it in a wooden cabinet in the department) and never wanted to see it or think about it again. I had been a hard worker and high achiever in school, but now I didn't understand what was going on or what I was writing about. The shame was deep.

I had come to Trinity with the wide-eyed naïveté of *Thoroughly Modern Millie* – moving to the big city to be inspired and have adventures. Instead, I was completely miserable, drowning in a sea of confusion and boredom. Luckily, I had a lifeline.

Two friends I knew who had started their own theatre company in Limerick were in the year above me. They urged me to audition for a show called *The Co-Op*. I had no idea what it was, only that the confident people at the stall had also urged me to get involved. So, I auditioned for the show during my first week, mainly because it filled an hour of my time.

Monday morning, I was headed back up to Dublin on the train at the last possible second. I remember walking through the front gates and seeing my name on the Players notice board amongst fifty other names. I was like an alien discovering humanity for the first time. Friends?

Our first rehearsal couldn't come soon enough. I counted down the minutes until finally I was crammed into the theatre space with dozens of other Freshers. The four directors stood up, quietened us down and gave us a dramatic and moving speech which went something like …

'Look around you. Amongst these people will be your maid of honour, your best man, your children's godparents, your partner, your lifelong friends.' That seemed a bit presumptive. I looked around at the sweaty, motley crew of weirdos and thought, no. No. These people are not for me.

They seemed unusual and loud and kind of annoying, and they talked a lot and loved theatre and I couldn't tell if what they were saying was a joke or they were doing a 'bit' or they were serious and loved performing. Oh, dear god, they love performing, and I think I just described myself.

The directors flopped around, loving being in charge. 'Okay, guys, seriously, listen up, this is important!' They led all fifty of us in games I had played as a child, and again I was confused. Wasn't this supposed to be a play? I sheepishly joined in, unbearably self-consciousness but happy I now had something to do in the evenings.

The general rule at Trinity is that people who were socially classified as nerds or dweebs in school get bumped up to cool status once they hit the Arts Block. Their skin clears up, puppy fat drops off and their unlimited knowledge of manga becomes alternative. That paired with a Players t-shirt and newfound confidence makes these people impossibly attractive. These were our four directors. They were who I longed to be. They knew everybody, were hilarious and played 'Zip-Zap-Bong!' with a wry irony that said, 'I know this is a child's game, what of it?' We all idolized them, 'we' here referring to the fifty cast members or minions they had selected to be part of the show.

By our second rehearsal, I was in heaven. Our first 'bonding' night out was in Spy – a club night for anyone who thought they were alternative or otherwise – which we frequented every week and was basically the coolest place I had ever been. 'Yeah, I go out to this night called Spy now?' I'd casually say to my friends back home in Limerick. Admittedly, I could feel a divide starting to form between me, the one who left, and them, the ones who stayed. And while

I missed the laughs we had while donning the fake tan and heels, I felt so much more at home in my clumpy boots and a second-hand jumper dancing on an old couch in Spy, absolutely ROASTING. I can still taste the 3 am €2 chicken fillet rolls we all queued for afterwards from Golden Centra. I wish I couldn't, but I can.

Our directors would lead us from place to place, rehearsals to night out to house party. And repeat every night for six weeks. I didn't know anyone, but I was best friends with everyone. It was the greatest time of my entire life.

I'm not exaggerating when I say that the show they wrote for us was the funniest thing I had ever seen or heard. My mind was blown during our first read-through, and it wasn't just the effect of the two cans I had downed as part of some game beforehand. I remember laughing the whole way through, and I was onstage.

'Corpsing' was another term that was new to me. It means laughing when you're not supposed to. One day I had an epiphany and realized I had been corpsing my entire young adult life. I was particularly prone to it during 'movement' classes or in lectures on performance art.

During this first read-through we were assigned our parts, and I had a solo which was the cause of a lot of drama between me and a new friend. She was annoyed she didn't get one too. These fights made sense at the time and seemed so devastating and important. Endless drunken chats in the toilet ensued. Long discussions and honesty over cigarettes under the awning outside the front door. Cigarettes for her, not me. Obviously, I was minding my throat since I had a solo …

Dramatics offstage like these were not uncommon around the Players building. People whispering on the stairwell or deep in conversation around the tatty brown couches in the theatre's front of house. Or those turning to face the noticeboard by the entrance to shield their steaming tears after a tactless break-up or, more likely, not getting the part they wanted. The drama of it all! Everything mattered so intensely, everything was high stakes. Except the performance itself, which wasn't really the point.

During those six weeks of nerve-wrecking rehearsals, countless messy nights out and millions of hilarious in-jokes, I began to finally feel at home in Players. My tribe was formed from this crazy, eccentric, gas group of humans, and I adored them. When the show was over, I rammed my schedule with back-to-back rehearsals for other plays, meetings and events. Suddenly I felt glad my course was only eight hours a week, I couldn't possibly fit another hour in.

My course continued, but I was kept busy with much more important matters like auditioning for the Director's Options – the shows made by fourth-year directing students that everyone wanted to be involved in – or discussing who would light design the twenty-four-hour musical. I was five minutes late for everything, rushing from venue to venue in order to pack it all in. Luckily, every place we used for rehearsals was within a two-minute running distance.

I could sprint up the numerous flights of stairs to the dance studio in under thirty seconds. That space was a gloriously wide and sunny room with windows overlooking the whole campus and another wall covered in mirrors. A door led out to the balcony for smoke breaks where directors would dramatically mull over how terribly rehearsals were going. It was where we didn't learn to dance, but certainly a lot of ambiguous 'movement' took place. This was supposed to be something to do with Drama and Theatre Studies too, but, like semiotics, the meaning of movement was lost on me for the first few years. I felt like it had nothing to do with acting.

This sunny movement studio was what I had envisioned Trinity facilities to look like. In reality, most of my days were spent rehearsing sketches and plays in the cold and windowless rooms called 191 or 192 – named after prison cells, or so I presumed. That's what they felt like from the inside.

On days when neither of those were free, we would brazenly rehearse in random lecture rooms in the Psychology building and be highly annoyed when we were kicked out, slumping out with faces that said, 'Don't they know we're rehearsing a play? We don't have time for this!' Meanwhile, the students of Introduction to Neuroscience and Behaviour looked on, deadpan and disinterested. I wonder why?

When I was on the DU Players' Committee we took matters, such as the use of the large, puce-coloured velvet couch which belonged in the rehearsal room as set in every play, very seriously. It was felt the use of the couch was bringing down the calibre of the productions since it appeared so frequently. The submissions process was also serious business. All twelve members of the committee would sit around a desk and grill applicants on their proposed play for the following term. I have been on both sides of this process and it's equally uncomfortable. The grillers would purposely try and catch the grilled out by asking them hard questions about their lighting designer, or, worse, bring up mistakes they had made in the past and ask them how they would prepare for that this time. Once everyone had been sufficiently intimidated, we would discuss the submissions ad nauseam. It was all very, very important.

Having worked in professional theatre for years now, I don't think I've ever experienced taking things as seriously as we did back then. Now, when a tech gets stressful or things aren't going to plan, there is always the bird's-eye view that 'hey, this is only theatre, it's supposed to be fun' or 'we're not getting paid enough to not enjoy this'. Whereas back then, it really felt like life or death. We would go round in circles, spending hours discussing the pros and cons of each submission before finally landing on the chosen twelve slots. Then we would order five wagon-wheel pizzas from Missoni's and pay for it from the Players budget.

Three years on from that first day at the Freshers' stall, suddenly I was the person telling fifty wide-eyed First Years to look around at the people in the room, how they would be their best men, their children's godparents, their life-long friends. As I repeated these seemingly saccharine words, I suddenly realized just how true they were. I looked across at my co-director and close friend, Paul, who, to this day, remains one of my closest friends. 'Just like me and Paul here,' I said mock-jokingly. The two of us looked at each other like we were satirizing a cheesy American film. Everyone laughed. They had to, we were the leaders. It was our turn.

When I gave that speech, Paul and I had been friends for three years. That seems like nothing now. We had experienced crazy nights out, many terrible and brilliant performances, grimy flat-shares and laughs. A decade on, we have grown up together. We have suffered through some of the hardest moments of adulthood, supporting each other through overwhelming periods of grief. I am so relieved we cemented the foundation of our friendship during those carefree Players days, because it has solidly been a support through some unbearably hard times since.

I am not denying I was an insufferable person during the four years I spent in that black box theatre. I knew nothing of the real world, and now that I do, I'm so grateful I had that time of ignorant bliss. I would be lying if I didn't say I really, really enjoyed every single minute of it. The completely oblivious self-importance was magical. The rare times I would come home, I bored my family with long anecdotes that ended with statements like 'it's just such bad form because the chair's play went to ISDA last year. So …' Deathly silence around the dinner table. Followed by questions like, 'Remind me, what is ISDA?' or 'Is the chair a person?' It was like I'd been adopted into a cult with our own secret language.

Rushed phone calls on the way to rehearsals replaced the forlorn texts I sent early on. If I hadn't called her in a particularly long time, my mother would glibly message me on Sundays asking, 'Are you still alive?' It wasn't passive-aggressive, she was genuinely just checking. I would text back 'Yes,' and she would reply 'X.' That was all she needed to know, so she was happy. As was I.

Erica Murray (TCD 2009–13; Drama and Theatre Studies) is a playwright and screenwriter from Co. Limerick. Her plays have been performed in Dublin, Belfast, Edinburgh and London. Her play **The Cat's Mother** won the Fishamble Award for New Writing and was nominated for the Stewart Parker Award.

In 2019, she was Artist In Residence at the Lyric Theatre in Belfast. She is currently working on a new play commission for Rough Magic Theatre Company and an original drama series for Drama Republic and Sky TV.

PLAYING

emma gleeson

They gave us the run of a theatre
Though we were just kids
Who liked to pretend.
Inside those black walls
We dreamt ourselves into being.
Tiger pups.
College-cossetted.
Interests unfurled
Fuelled by chicken fillet rolls.

Lights hung and lines learnt
We wove something
Bigger than the sum of parts.
Late nights sowed seeds
That now spring forth
Lives lived in the service of stories
Each of us a spoke
Spinning out from
One slapdash source

Bonds forged
In that furnace
Of self-creation
Of all-day-togetherness
Of shared discovery
Well, they've proven hard to shake.
And though edges frayed
Behind busy laughter
We were as well to skip
The Greek theatre lectures.
We'd found catharsis in each other.

DU Players committee, 2008. From left, standing: *Colm McNally, Ross Dungan, Ciaran Clarke, Manus Halligan, Zia Bergin-Holly, Sam McMullan, Sarah Duffy and Barry McStay.* From left, kneeling and seated: *Emma Gleeson, Pauline McLynn and Matt Smyth.*

Emma Gleeson (TCD 2006–10; Drama and Theatre Studies) is a writer and sustainability activist based in Dublin. After finishing her undergraduate studies at Trinity, she completed an MA in the History and Culture of Fashion at the London College of Fashion. Her first book, **Stuff Happens!**, was published by Penguin Sandycove in March 2021. She delivers corporate workshops and is a frequent media contributor on sustainability, ethical fashion and consumer culture. Her poems have featured in Leaving Cert textbooks and **Poethead**, and can be found at droppingslow.com

WHAT'S IN A NAME?

jess majekodunmi

MY NAME IS Majekodunmi.

It holds eleven letters and five Yoruba words. It translates into Irish as *Ná lig dó mé a ghortú*. It extends from the one who was named first through four generations to me. It evokes pride and pain and purpose. It contains at least three TCD graduates, and carries the single reason I applied to Trinity in the first place.

//

My name set its course for Trinity College Dublin in 1935 aboard a boat from Lagos to Dublin via Takoradi, Freetown, Monrovia and Liverpool. Almost seventy years before I graduated from Trinity, Moses Majekodunmi became the first of my name to attend TCD.

Moses the first is my mother's father's father's uncle's son. Between his birth in 1916 and boarding the Harland & Wolff-built passenger liner *M.V. Apapa* in 1935, Moses did many things and many things were done to him, all documented in the first twenty pages of his autobiography, which can be found getting dusty out in Santry Stacks.

The second chapter is all about his time at Trinity. He describes disembarking in the early hours and making his way through deserted Dublin streets to his lodging on Baggot Street, and his first impression of Trinity College.

He writes with a familiar familial *pernicketyness* of precision that would have impressed Joyce:

> You approach the College through an area known as College Green which is a misnomer because by the time I entered college in 1935, there was no 'green' in sight. The place had given way to a busy business centre with the Bank of Ireland on one side of the square and numerous insurance houses on the other side. Leading away from the 'green' is Grafton Street, famous for all the most fashionable shops in Ireland. You enter the College grounds through a massive iron gate into a small courtyard on either side of which are the impressive statues of Edmund Burke and Oliver Goldsmith … This courtyard leads through Regent House to the Front Square, the centre of gravity of the College.

Standing in that same courtyard, clasped by the weightiness of its gravity, I made my decision to come to Trinity College when I was ten years old.For so long I have romanticized this recollection that now I reluctantly question it.

Moses Majekodunmi receiving an Honorary Doctorate Degree in Law (LLD)
from Trinity College Dublin, 1964.

I will concede it is easily possible I could have been eight, or thirteen. Even so, I clearly remember standing on the cobbles and simply deciding. It is the cobbles that make the memory so distinct, definite. Cobblestones are memorable because they seem to hold memory, worn down by having so much to remember.

We were over from England visiting our cousins, like we did every summer. Every summer I heard stories of the Leonards on Francis Street and Majekodunmis in Trinity, of dances in The Gresham and meeting dates at Nelson's Pillar, of the aunties who lived above The Dubliner restaurant on Francis Street and of the uncles working at the Mater and the Rotunda. My Irish and Nigerian heritage both intertwined around Dublin landmarks, the stories inseparable. And so I followed this inevitable path to those cobblestones – attending the university of my forefathers, in the city of my foremothers.

I chose the college, not the course. Without too much deliberation, I limited my options to the alma mater of the Majekodunmi. With a sentimental stubbornness, I didn't consider anywhere else apart from Trinity. And to be sure, I applied for three different courses. An accident of grades and the advantage of a name decided which. Basically, my A-level flush of Bs wasn't good enough for the first round of offers. With the impending prospect of a daughter with crushed dreams, my mum reached out to a family friend who knew someone who was a professor in Trinity. He was persuaded to look into it, and came back saying the Majekodunmi name was recognized, just hold on for the second round of offers. We duly waited, and I was offered a place to study English. An offer solidifying the bind between Trinity and Majekodunmis and me. It's a truth that at the time I was most grateful for, even proud perhaps. Now I'm embarrassed, even ashamed. A nepotistic privilege that I didn't deserve. My name got me in. And, feck it, I'm so glad. Oh, the wonky, faux-idealistic morals of an English student.

//

My aunt wrote me a card from England. It had been more than thirty years since she had lived as a child in Drimnagh and went to Ardscoil Éanna in Crumlin. She said I was the first of us to move back home. A godmotherly nod of approval for my repatriation. My grandfather wrote me a letter from Lagos. It had been more than fifty years since he had lived and studied in Dublin – although not at Trinity. Bobo was just up the road at the Royal College of

Surgeons, a college I dismissed due to not studying medicine. (Moses no doubt would have appreciated how it is on a green that is actually a green.) Bobo was very concerned about prejudice I might face attending Trinity, and articulated to me with his concerns in a letter:

> How are you settling down in Trinity College Dublin, T.C.D.? I hope there is religious tolerance there? I mean, I hope they tolerate Roman Catholicism. In the early fifties of the century just gone out, I heard a Priest announcing in the Roman Catholic Church in Dublin, that Roman Catholics must not send their children to Trinity College Dublin.

Although he later converted to Catholicism, at the time Bobo was a Protestant and knew Trinity well, eating his afternoon meals at the buffet. I don't know if he would have seen himself as a minority. In his letters, he describes himself plainly as a Nigerian student in 1950s Dublin, or, more specifically, 'in my time the population of Nigerian students, excluding all other Africans and African descendants, was between 300 and 450'. (Recognize that familial pernicketyness of precision?)

For me, it wasn't religion or race that posed questions of tolerance – it was nationality.

I didn't understand why most people studying English at Trinity were, well, English. I notice this immediately and it really narked me. If I'd wanted to study English literature with English people, I would have applied to study English in England. So much for returning home.

They weren't just English though, they were a southern, public-school-kids type of English. Growing up in Stoke, I'd heard of their type. In my mind at the time, they were the very worst England had to offer. Somehow, they all seemed connected, their parents all knew each other's parents. Somehow, I was completely disconnected. None of them knew my parents, none of them even knew a Majekodunmi. And this web of connection congealed their identity in my mind, a silky mass of privilege and RP accents. With a sweeping judgment, I branded them all as posh kids. Obviously, this was massively unfair of me, and ridiculously disparaging.

Even with a top-notch secondary-school education and a few elocution lessons thrown in, my vowels gave me away. I say 'up' like 'ughp' not 'ahp'. They heard it like a northern klaxon. Freshers introductions went something like this:

'You're not from London.'

'No, Stoke.'

'Where would that be? Ahp north somewhere?'

'Yeah, between Manchester and Birmingham.'

'Where did you go to school?'

'Stoke.'

'Oh. Where's your surname from?'

'Nigeria.'

'I boarded with a Nigerian prince.'

'I'm Irish actually.'

'Really.'

Really.

To me, this confrontation of class was confusing. The conversations barely stopped short of articulating the Lock Stock dividing lines of 'southern fairies' and 'northern monkeys'. How did I end up in this situation, justifying what lies north of the Watford gap, in Dublin? To them, I was confusing. All the standard markers of an identity uniform – my name, my accent, my nationality, my colour – were mismatched. One thing we all knew, I was most definitely not English like them.

I grew up on a cul-de-sac in Stoke-on-Trent with my mum and grandma. Me and my mates were at the bottom end. There was a shared little green, and jumpers did make good goalposts. I remember the kids at the top end – we didn't hang out with them much, they were a bit older – asking me 'Are you a paki?' Honestly, I had absolutely no idea. I had a fifty–fifty chance of getting it right, but perhaps I detected the heaviness of the question and even those odds seemed risky. So off I ran inside to consult my grandma. She set me straight and I marched back outside, proud to have a confident answer. 'I'm not a paki, I'm Irish.' They shrugged, 'Okay then.' And that was that. It was easier to be accepted as Irish in a council estate in Stoke than it was as a student in Trinity College Dublin.

If only I could find someone from Dublin in Trinity, we could reminisce about summer months in sunny Wexford, building sandcastles on Morriscastle beach and the chips from the chippers in Kilmuckridge.

If only I could find an Irish classmate who saw me as Irish like them.

I don't have freckles. I don't have red hair. I don't burn on sunny days drinking cans by the canal. I don't sound like a Dub, Northsider or Southsider. I inherited the Majekodunmi name of my grandfather and not the Leonard of my grandmother. Sure, how am I to show I'm Irish? How else can I express it, except with the words 'I'm Irish'?

When I moved to Dublin in 2000, I put tins in the press and knew that lemonade was either red or white, yet I called runners 'trainers' and had never seen the *Late Late*. How many cultural references are enough to overcome my voice? My eyes are green. Is that enough without the white skin? Maybe it is through them alone that I can see and be seen.

At least I had the books. Studying was a pendulum of fascinating lectures and boring lectures. And lots of reading, so much reading. I chose the most non-English English Studies options possible: Anglo-Irish and Post-Colonial, hyphenated labels to encompass the multitudes. Yeats said things fall apart, and so did Achebe. The Palm-Wine Drinkard teamed up with The Quare Fellow. Reading about identity, seminars about identity, forming identity, protecting identity, seeking identity. Ridiculously clichéd, isn't it? Eighteen years old and figuring out identity.

Steph Newell brought in a kola nut for us to touch. She recognized my name and asked questions. Back then, I'd never been to Nigeria and I had few answers. My name on paper masked a fraudulence. My name in person demanded interrogation.

Not proper English. Not proper Irish. Not proper Nigerian. Between what I look like and what I feel, how I grew up and how I show up, it is a twisted identity pantomime trap. Oh yes I am. Oh no you're not. Or maybe half of me is and half of me isn't. I reacted against it all, all these proof points of what I was not.

//

My cousin Dapo wrote his autobiography in 1996, forty years after arriving in Dublin on the boat from England, where he had lived and schooled for many years:

> The crossing to Dublin was quite an experience. The friendly warmth
> of the Irish was striking. Everybody talked to one another during the

crossing of the Irish sea. The non-Irish were not excluded, everybody drank freely. When the Irish mountain was seen at the horizon, the Irish came to attention and sang the Irish national anthem in Irish. This show of Irish nationalism and friendliness so impressed me that I decided that if ever I had children they would study in Dublin.

Yet another family literary work laden with a pernicketyness of precision and sentimental stubbornness. (He kept his word, his four children all did.)

In 1956, Irish universities welcomed direct applications from students, whereas England, Dapo's home at that time, operated a quota system for 'colonial students'. Of all the medical schools in Ireland, he chose Trinity for the same reason I did – because of Moses the first, because of our name.

I remember Dapo well. Firstly, because he had the same birthday as me. For a child, this was quite an extraordinary revelation. And secondly because he was the only person Grandma would let sit in her chair. He'd just appear in our house sometimes – regularly enough for his arrival to not be a surprise, but infrequent enough for his visit to be a cause for excitement. Dapo and Grandma would talk for hours, they'd known each other since the 50s and their days in Dublin.

Moses, Bobo and Dapo all had lives away from their studies. Moses reminisced of meeting De Valera and Alfie Byrne, going to the Gate Theatre and meeting Nora, his wife-to-be. In his letters to me, Bobo yearned for the Dodder as 'the river that watered the affection and romance between Ann (your grandmother) and my poor self. We strolled hand in hand in the cool of the evenings, under the moonlight, along that river'. Meanwhile Dapo was making 'important discoveries like the four provinces Dance Hall, Davy Byrnes Bar, Crystal Ballroom, Metropole Ballroom for Sunday afternoon relaxation (Sunday school) and Cleary's Ballroom'.

Between 2000 and 2004, I too made important discoveries. I fell in love with the person I'm still in love with today, worked backstage on the ill-fated Eamon Dunphy TV show, did an internship with *The Dubliner* magazine, collected empty pint glasses in Mother Reilly's, qualified as an FAI referee, volunteered with the Special Olympics, danced in Toast and watched Shirley Temple Bar on Telly Bingo. Trinity was only ever part of my existence, like my name is not my whole story.

//

To Moses, Dapo and Bobo:

What's in our name? Is it a metaphor? An imperative? A plea? An explanation?

In so many ways, you three deeply influenced my time and memories of Trinity, even though none of you were in Dublin at the same time as me. Our name, written on a cobbled palimpsest.

It holds eleven letters and five Yoruba words. It translates into Irish as *Ná lig dó mé a ghortú.* Don't let it pain me.

Photo credit: Ruth Medjber.

Jess Majekodunmi (TCD 2000–4; English Studies) is a design historian and an innovation designer, and is OK with contradictions. Since graduating from Trinity, her career has zig-zagged across continents, roles and sectors, including for-profit and non-profit organizations. Jess is a co-founding member of Beyond Representation, an organization championing women of colour who are breaking new ground in Irish media, arts and business. Jess says she tries to be fearless when battling imposter syndrome and gracious when asked where she is from.

POPULAR LITERATURE

adam crothers

1

The Nightmare by Fuseli is scraping the fuselage
from the inside of the monkey-barrel out. The coffin
contained, but for the scratches and miasma, utter zilch.
Purely platonic, the love betwixt nightshade and cave-in.

Impurely agapic, the fizzing distance from the heart
to that which squats thereon. Lines' lateral thought; their ludic
– as those who don't play say – tightening of a neural thread
(or, if one insists, their tightening of a more lo-tech

equivalent such as the obscure band on a trilby,
the tentacular grip of a quite believable god,
or a screw in the tape deck of a crap surveillance drone),

the prime hope being to snag the fang-mark of an earlobe,
the callus of a forefinger, or the tongue-tip that blagged
its way through the odd seminar but not the odder one.

2

The odder one of the twins: not the one to watch out for.
Tough, though, to rank oddness, having become, in this order,
drunk on hemlock, Porlock, ether, Lethe's waters, ether
(at which a pause to confirm they all see what happened there),

and the goblin fruit of conflating Lethe and Liffey,
which is old news, and so won't make it into the poem,
lest the twice-bedevilled vision deriving from Le Fa-
nu's offer of green tea lower into the shot the boom

on which I've left more prints than a carbon Machiavel,
loading the deck, an Alice Liddell positively wreathed
in the vampire who's noted, via jugular fiddle,

that her blood clothes a clot sized for the dot in the 'M.Phil'
on the transcript of a nanobot whose every thought
looms large as the cherry fedora on that femme fatale.

3

The cherry fedora on that femme fatale is tying
itself in knots trying to adjust the faders that fade,
in a better world, the worse world out and the better in.
This is terrible terrain. This is uphill. This is void

if removed from allegedly common experience.
The monkey-barrel's unlikely faster-than-light commute
clatters across the keys: a few million aspirins,
in the space of one aspiration, sprinting the gamut

from plot outline to gut. Even the tormented scion
stalking secret ancestral passageways maligns and hates
less than the hollow text that each night raises, disrobing,

a toast to the variety of flame that fans fictions
into falsehoods, with a caustic air that exacerbates
the itch at which *The Nightmare* by Fuseli is scraping.

Adam Crothers (TCD 2005–6; MPhil Popular Literature) was born in Belfast in 1984 and works in an academic library in Cambridge. He studied at Trinity on the MPhil in Popular Literature, 2005–6. His two books of poems are **Several Deer** (Carcanet, 2016), which in 2017 won the Shine/Strong Poetry Award and the Seamus Heaney Centre Prize, and **The Culture of My Stuff** (Carcanet, 2020); he's at work on the next two, and on a novel (a space opera).

COBBLESTONE AMBIVALENCE

caitríona lally

IN 2017, I spoke at an event about my experiences as a student and as a cleaner in Trinity College. The chair of the panel, Gerald Dawe, asked if I considered myself a 'Trinity writer'. Conscious of the graduates in the audience – a mix of old and middle-aged people who seemed to hold onto this Trinity connection so firmly – I fumbled, trying to avoid the question directly, but Dawe persisted. He named several writers who had gone to the university and written about it and asked if I felt part of this contingent. I finally said no, I didn't see myself as a Trinity writer.

My relationship to Trinity is similar to that of a distant family member I have a slightly troubled connection with. Some of the audience members talked of college with a capital C, living in Rooms with a capital R. They dropped definite articles, added capital letters, spoke the lingo of the tribe with ease. Until I was asked to that event, I had never thought too deeply about Trinity. It was where I did my degree, and now it was where I took my weekly paycheque from. But my memories were not rosy-simple, sepia-tinged ones.

My time in Trinity wasn't as immersive as that of some other students. I lived at home during my student years, which diluted the college experience. I didn't fling myself wholeheartedly into the student clubs and societies. I disliked the college's insular bubble of Trinity and couldn't understand why you would have coffee in the college and drink in the college bar when we were in the middle of town and could do that outside in the real world. I have a particular phobia of cliques and sets that reek of exclusivity and belonging; where there's a tribe there's outsiders. Trinity was part of my life, but not my life.

In 1997, when I did my Leaving Cert, the only place to study Clinical Speech and Language Studies in the Republic was Trinity, so that's where I went. I was eighteen before I ever set foot in the college; I hadn't realized non-students could walk through the grounds, and I hadn't gone to the Trinity open day while I was in secondary school. Even though I was from a background in which the prospect of going on to third-level education was no stretch, the solid mass of Trinity lobbed in the middle of College Green seemed too daunting a fortress to enter.

I was lucky enough to get through college at a time when third-level education was almost free, when the registration fee ran to the low hundreds and not to the thousands – an odiously dishonest way to sneak fees back in while claiming free education. This meant I could drop out of my speech therapy course after two years, disillusioned with my inability to instantly cure lisps and stutters. (I was a very naïve teenager who hadn't really understood the *therapy* part of the course.) I also felt able to start over and study English, which, if fees were as high as they are today, I might not have done. I probably would have chosen a vocational course that gave me a better chance of employment instead of an eight-hours-of-lectures-a-week course chosen for the sheer pleasure of reading. The privilege and luxury of that was not wasted on me, maybe because I was a bit older than my peers. I had worked a couple of dogsbody jobs in my year out between courses, and had experienced the high-pressure schedule of nine-to-five lectures plus assignments on my speech therapy course, with little scope for imagination.

My mother had gone to UCD and liked to tell me tales of how at Trinity they used to shoot Catholic priests on sight. When the neighbours asked where I went to college, she'd blush awkwardly and mutter that I was studying 'somewhere in town', which had people wondering where or what I was studying that was so mortifying.

Most of my friends at the time were not Trinity students; they went to various colleges or DITs or none. There was good-natured (I think) piss-taking about the arrogance of Trinity students among us. A friend attending DIT Kevin Street would roar, 'Trinners for Winners!' at me. A UCD friend used to send me those chainmail jokes that were popular in the early days of email, of the 'how-many-Trinity-students-does-it-take-to-change-a-lightbulb?' variety. (One: she holds the bulb and the world revolves around her.) We would gate-crash whichever college student nights sounded like the most craic. There were céilís and traffic-light balls. It was an enviably carefree time in which the most pressing decision was whether to wear green or orange at the traffic-light ball. At one Romeo and Juliet ball, I was given a Ginger Rogers sticker and went looking for my Fred Astaire, but when I saw the cut of Fred vomiting in a corner, I quickly ripped off my sticker. This was a time before cut-price drinks promotions were outlawed and we got drunk on nothing, the pure giddy fun of late teens.

My decision to change courses was heavily influenced by a trip to UCD. I used to go to Belfield to run on the track or meet friends, and one day I sat in on a friend's English lecture. Even though I was only killing time until he was free to go to lunch, I couldn't stop myself taking notes on *Robinson Crusoe*. Slowly it dawned on me that you could study make-believe instead of learning stern, brute facts and regurgitating them for exams. I could read things that were the invention of someone's imagination and form opinions about them myself. So, UCD English sent me back to Trinity English. The decision was simple: UCD at the time had no pure English degree, and Trinity was in town, meaning just one bus, an important factor when taking nine o'clock lectures into consideration.

I studied English from 2000 to 2004. It took me a while to get into my stride, about four years if I'm honest. It was a completely different world to what I was used to. On the first day, I was astonished by various Dublin students with Ross O'Carroll-Kelly accents asking which school I went to. I was even more bewildered when, on hearing the unfamiliar name of my local secondary school, they retreated so hastily that smoke was practically coming from their shoes. This seemed to me the height of not just exclusivity but paro-chiality. In the early 2000s, there were many British students in the class, some of whom had gone to the kind of schools the royal family and British MPs attend, the kind of schools that made the Dublin fee-paying schools seem like poverty-stricken backwaters. I felt like I was on the set of *Brideshead Revisited* listening to the double barrels of names so polysyllabic they seemed quadruple-barrelled. I can't emphasize enough what a foreign world this was to me. Here were students who had got As in A-level English and had read so widely, and dropped so many literary and philosophical references into their conversation, that I felt like a toddler who hadn't yet learned to read.

I like small talk – no talk is too small for me – but when I would try to chat about the weather or other innocuous topics to students in tutorials, they looked disdainful. Their discussions were highbrow, intellectual, and if I hadn't even *heard of*, never mind *read* the thinkers and philosophers they talked of, it was a struggle to find an in to the conversation. The points they found in the prescribed reading that in their eyes became a New Historicist/Marxist/post-structuralist comment on society, where did they find those things? Were we reading the same books at all? I was so confounded I sat silent in tutorials for four years, terrified I'd be called on to offer up my tepid takes on the prescribed text.

I was lamenting my failure to participate in discussions to my parents one day when they came up with a solution: read the book in question thoroughly, prepare one point you want to make, then as soon as the tutorial starts, lash your point into the conversation and sit back, job done. I took their advice and went into the tutorial, bursting with my single point, but before I could muster up the courage to open my mouth, another student made an infinitely more insightful observation which sent the discussion in a completely different direction. I stared at my one point, but the more I looked at it, the more lack-lustre, prosaic and downright dumb it seemed. I attempted my dad's second piece of advice: think like a politician and twist the conversation around to the point you want to make. It would have required gargantuan leaps to manipulate my superficial point in the direction the tutorial was going. No matter how agile my brain was or how many mental contortions I pulled, my prepared comment was destined for obsolescence.

It was the ease of the students from colossally privileged backgrounds that struck me – their ability to swagger into a room and talk about any subject with confidence, even if it took me four years to realize that much of what they said was either lifted directly from secondary texts or utter drivel dressed up in an impressive vocabulary. A student I remember used to lounge in tutorials almost horizontal with confidence, arms behind his head, feet on the table, the ease of his sprawl reminiscent of Jacob Rees-Mogg at that infamous Brexit debate.

I was three years older than most of the other students, but instead of giving me extra confidence, it made me feel like the kid in school who's a foot taller than the others, having stayed back a few years because she wasn't quite getting it. In a tutorial in my final year, one of the more confident students – let's call him Tarquin Pinklesworth Montgomery Bluffington – leaned back in his chair and spewed forth on the play we were talking about. The words from his mouth were very insightful, in-depth, relevant and … directly lifted from the introduction to the same obscure edition to the play I had! I was equal parts horrified and relieved – these were not his own original thoughts, but he was passing them off as such. And if I wasn't so foolishly naïve and self-sabotagingly honest I should have learned a valuable life lesson from that; the people who get on in the world are often those who rob others' ideas and pass them off as their own with the bluster of a Brexit politician.

If all this sounds a bit ranty, it shouldn't. I enjoyed my four years in college, confidence crisis notwithstanding. I made good friends and I loved the reading. I just felt like I didn't fit in. The fact that I felt so intimidated wasn't the fault of Trinity College, the institution. Maybe I just didn't have that much in common with the people who so desperately wanted to be Trinity students, what my friends and I called the 'Cobblestone Complex' – the desire to go to Trinity at all costs. I was never made to feel inferior by lecturers, there was just an underlying sense of privilege and assumptions among a certain sector of the Arts Block – that you had gone to a fee-paying school, that you never had to earn your own money. In fairness, it wasn't as if these students had consciously looked down on me; it was more that they didn't look on me at all, being single-barrelled and invisible, with possibly too much bog in my accent. I remember coming across an extraordinarily posh girl from my tutorial group in a shop in town. When I greeted her, she blanked me so thoroughly I thought she had difficulties with her hearing or vision, but when I said 'HI' louder and added a wave, it was clear she was deliberately ignoring me. I was more bemused than hurt; it still intrigues me that a grown human would be so ignorant to someone from outside their set.

If I was articulate and confident speaking up in a crowd, none of this would have mattered. I would probably have quivered mutely in a DIT or NUI tutorial, because I'm not a natural speaker nor do I hold the floor with ease.

Some students came from backgrounds so privileged they didn't have to work in summer. They spent their summers 'reading ahead'. Their parents covered the rent for their apartments in Dublin while they read the reading list for the upcoming academic year and, presumably, sat around with other non-working students, discussing what they'd read. *Wow.* I worked babysitting and house-cleaning jobs during the year and spent summers with Trinity housekeeping. The college takes on students to spring-clean the student residences and then to clean for the tourists who stay in the summer. When I found myself unemployed eleven years after graduating, I returned to work in Trinity housekeeping, spending the first nine months as a spare, cleaning wherever was needed.

The job I dreaded most was cleaning the rooms of the debating societies after their club events. The food and drink mess was so pervasive it seemed deliberately done, and it reminded me of the overprivileged idiots having food fights at the Gentlemen's Club in *Jeeves and Wooster* because, obviously, the help will clean it up. It made me think of that apocryphal tale of the Oxbridge admissions interview in which prospective students were given cherries to eat and those who threw the stones on the floor were accepted, having demonstrated they were used to having servants to clean up their messes.

Certain events stand out from my time in Trinity. When George W. Bush was elected US president after the recount in 2000, I remember the shock among classmates. An extremely posh lad who would never usually have noticed me initiated a conversation about it; an event of such international significance was a great equalizer. At the time, we thought Bush was just a dolt in the White House, little knowing what a dangerous dolt he was. Sixteen years and four elections later, I experienced echoes of this same shock when I clocked in for my cleaning job at the security desk in Trinity the morning Donald Trump was elected. I huddled over the newsfeed with cleaners and security guards in dread. I was pregnant at the time and frightened at the sort of world I was bringing a baby into: another dangerous dolt in the White House.

The September 11th attacks happened during my time in college, but as Trinity used to start term in October, we were scattered when they took place.

After our return to college, the talk was of what Bush would do to retaliate, and this mobilized students. We marched in the anti-Iraq War demonstration in Dublin in 2003. I'd been on protests before, but this felt different, so big it might actually achieve something. It achieved nothing.

Some lecturers were particularly memorable, like the Greek drama professor who would stride into the classroom in a black cloak bellowing ancient Greek verse, handing out readings in the ancient Greek alphabet which none of us could read and talking casually about the characters' bouts of pederasty. The enthusiastic lecturer who taught us Old English and alleviated our terror of exam translations with pretzels, an exotic treat in Ireland two decades ago. And Amanda Piesse, my first-year tutor who wrote a note on the bottom of one of my essays in First Year to come see her. It was the single most important event of my student life. Amanda walked me through my essay, line by line, showing me how I could improve my overly informal style to third-level standards, and reassured me that I had as much to say as the more vocal students. I think Amanda was kind to waifs and strays, and this waif would likely have strayed if it wasn't for her.

I met a former lecturer recently who asked me if there was a twenty-year reunion. I winced and tried to explain how intimidated I had felt by my fellow students. She said Trinity had changed a lot, that there was more awareness of access and inclusivity now, which was reassuring, but the idea of paying to meet people who'd ghosted me was absurd. I hope it's a more welcoming place to study these days. My background was as solidly boring middle-class as you can get, and if I felt intimidated, I can only imagine how someone from a less privileged background felt.

During my student years, I had no clue what I wanted to do career-wise. My eye was on going to live in Japan after graduating, rather than further study, and the idea of writing a book didn't cross my mind until my thirties. I didn't put in my time at one of the university papers, I took up my parchment on graduating, frantically trying to find linguistic scholars to translate Latin for my future boss in Japan to prove I had graduated.

When my first novel was published in 2015, I needed an author's bio, but I had zero publications to my name, no short story or essay credits to mention. I wrote that I studied English in Trinity, and this wasn't changed in later editions.

So, for all my claimed ambivalence, my novel bio boasts to anyone who reads it that I went to Trinity. And that sets me up nicely for another Trinity joke. When someone asks where you went to college, you say Trinity. Then they ask: 'How do you know someone went to Trinity?' They tell you.

Caitríona Lally's (TCD 1997–9, Clinical Speech and Language Studies; 2000–4, English Studies) first novel, **Eggshells**, was published in 2015. She won the 2018 Rooney Prize for Irish Fiction and the 2019 Lannan Literary Fellowship for Fiction. Her second novel, **Wunderland**, will be published by New Island in 2021. She lives in Dublin with her partner and their two small children.

DULYN

heledd fychan

SEPTEMBER 1999, and I was standing on the deck of the HSS ferry making the journey from my native Wales to Dublin. Holyhead was fast disappearing into the distance, and for the first time nerves kicked in and it struck me – *I don't know anybody in Ireland, and this is now going to be my home.*

My parents were travelling with me, and we had a car full of stuff. They sensed my nerves and reminded me that my home in Anglesey was closer to Dublin than it was to Cardiff – only ninety-nine minutes away on the fast ferry compared to the five hours by train or car to reach the Welsh capital. Though this was reassuring, the fact remained that we would be separated by the sea, and I would be using a different currency and language, making it seem like a much bigger move than if I'd stayed in Wales.

From Dún Laoghaire, we travelled to Rathmines and to my new home. Trinity Hall was not as it is now. This was pre-redevelopment, and the old house was the most prominent building. I'm sure today's students would be horrified by the décor and the very basic facilities we had at the time. But I instantly loved my ground-floor room in Cunningham House with its bed, desk and sink, and I began unpacking. Slowly but surely others started arriving, before we eventually said farewell to our parents and headed to the pub to start bonding.

And that's when the first challenge arose. My first language is Welsh, and I was brought up in a Welsh-speaking area and within a Welsh-speaking family. All my education up to that point had been through the medium of Welsh, and though I understood and wrote well in English, I had never really had to use it in an informal environment. I had a very strong Welsh accent, and it was clear that my new acquaintances were struggling to understand me. But they weren't the only ones having difficulty. Though I had no problem understanding the majority, I had never before encountered the Northern Ireland accent and could not understand what this tall, striking girl called Nicola from Armagh was saying to me. But I knew instantly that once the language barriers were overcome, we'd become firm friends.

I was lucky to have a space in Halls, as it meant I had company walking through Front Arch on the first day of Freshers' Week. I remember the excitement of seeing all of the society stands lined up, and students trying to persuade us to join. I signed up to far too many and got caught up in the excitement of it all. As someone who'd done a lot of debating, I was instantly drawn to the Hist. I was told to come along to the GMB and take part in a debate, but just as I was about to move onto another stand, one of the members said to me that I'd need to tone down my accent if anybody was to take me seriously and laughed in my face. With my confidence dented, that was the beginning and the end of my relationship with the Hist, though I did enjoy attending some events organized by the society during my time at Trinity.

Much of the social activities are a bit of a blur, but I remember having a lot of fun during that first week in the Buttery Bar and attending Freshers' nights in various establishments around Dublin, including Pegs and the Palace. I won a Smirnoff Ice watch and hat during one of the events and continued to bond with the girls from Trinity Hall. And, of course, there were the practical things to do like setting up a Bank of Ireland account, and availing of their free phone offer for students.

Whilst at school, I had always had a mixed-gender group of friends, and it struck me during that first week how petrified both sexes seemed to be of one another. One of my new friends explained to me the reason for her nervousness stemmed from going to an all-girls school and never before properly mixing with boys. It tuned out that this was true for the majority, and whilst my female friends in Wales were calling me with news of their adventures with the opposite sex during Freshers' Week, our fun in Dublin was much more innocent.

Naïvely, I also had not appreciated before moving to Ireland the role religion continued to play in society. As a child of the 80s, I was of course familiar with the Troubles in Northern Ireland and the bombings in England. I had been in the exact spot that was bombed in Manchester in 1996 a week prior to the bombing, and thought I understood the issues. But I also thought that my generation would be different and was surprised to be asked what religion I was when a member of the opposite sex finally approached me for a chat one evening. I explained that I had been christened as a Methodist – like the majority of Wales – but that I wasn't particularly religious. He invited me to a party the following night, and I accepted the offer.

Walking into the party, I was greeted by a huge picture of Margaret Thatcher and I asked the boy who'd invited me if that was their dartboard. The mood suddenly turned, and he asked me if I was a Unionist.

I explained that I was a member of Plaid Cymru and supported an independent Wales. His mind was blown. He had no idea that you could be a Protestant and a nationalist, and we quickly agreed that it would be better for everyone if I left. We exchanged polite nods whenever we ran into each other at Trinity, but never again spoke.

Another question that came up a lot during those first few weeks was which school did you go to and how many points did you get in your Leaving Cert? My course – History and Political Science – had only fourteen places available that year, and one or two of my fellow classmates were desperate to know who had the highest points. They had obviously been high achievers in their schools and wanted to be top dog in their new environment. They hated when I or one of the other students in the class did better than them, and they treated many of our assignments as competitions, though the majority of us had no interest in joining in.

I had always loved history, but I truly fell in love with the subject during my first year. Dr Sean Duffy's course – Ireland, Scotland and Wales in the Middle Ages – was the first time I had ever had an opportunity to properly study Welsh history, and he often called on me to pronounce the names of the various Welsh princes and place names. For my A-level course in Wales, we had studied the Tudors and the European Reformation, and to this day people are campaigning in Wales for Welsh history to be taught in schools. Dr Duffy could definitely teach the Welsh government a thing or two about how history should be incorporated into the curriculum!

Not all of his teaching methods were conventional. As one of our lectures was at the end of the day, it occasionally moved to the Thing Mote pub on Suffolk Street, where he would relay to us the history of the Vikings in Dublin, bringing it all to life. Those were undoubtedly some of my favourite classes.

Dr Terry Barry also took us outside of the walls of Trinity. Though some of the trips were to look at medieval castles, others were post-lecture catch-ups at Dunne & Crescenzi, where we would discuss history but also chat about day-to-day life. I was fortunate that he was my personal tutor and ended up being someone I turned to a lot for advice during my time at Trinity. He even forgave me during my final year for falling asleep during a Friday afternoon lecture where we were in a darkened and warm room looking at slides of castles. I reassured him that it wasn't a reflection of his teaching but rather the result of a late night in Doyle's the previous night!

Though I enjoyed the political science element of my course and have nothing but praise for my lecturers, my relationship was very different with the department compared to that of history. Class sizes were bigger, and tutorials were much more intense and serious. I learnt a lot, but felt like one of many rather than part of the department.

That first year was very much an introduction to Dublin and to Ireland – understanding the difference between the north and south side, appreciating the beauty of the Brown Thomas windows at Christmas and enjoying the *Late Late Show* – in particular the annual *Late Late Toy Show*. Understanding that 'feck' could be said at any time during the day on radio and television and wasn't considered swearing, that Temple Bar is only really for tourists and, if you want a late-night drink, then Leeson Street is the place to go.

By Second Year, I was ready to get more involved in college life, and with the encouragement of my classmate Alison from Dundalk I put my name forward to become class rep. This created quite a bit of tension, as the person who had done the role the previous year wanted to carry on. He was not happy, and made this very clear to me. But with quiet encouragement from others, I put in my nomination and was elected.

My increased involvement in different societies coincided with a massive personal change during my second year, when I lost over seven stone in weight over the course of eleven months. I had always been overweight, and the weight had piled on even more during my first year. The pictures from my first Trinity Ball horrified me, and I knew I needed to take action.

This was helped by the fact that by Second Year I was living in a lovely but tiny flat in Rathmines with Wendy, a kind-hearted girl with the most beautiful smile from Cong. We had hit it off in halls and decided to live together, which we then did for the remainder of our time as undergraduates. We cooked for one another, and she supported my weight-loss efforts, even joining me in doing a weird vegetable detox over the course of one weekend.

As the weight fell off, my confidence grew, and by my third year I was also the Students' Union convenor for Arts and Humanities and involved in Trinity FM and *Miscellany* magazine. I finally felt part of the student community and extended my friendship group beyond my Trinity Hall network and class-mates. Whilst the Hist had been unwelcoming and daunting, House 6 become a haven for me and somewhere I could finally be myself. It was a huge honour when I was elected Education Officer in 2003, and my year as a sabbatical officer was amongst the best of my life. This was largely due to the fact that I was part of an officer team that included Annie Gatling as President and Katie Dickson as Deputy President, both of whom remain close friends and are a constant source of inspiration.

For my final year at Trinity and during my year as a sabbatical officer, I was fortunate enough to live on campus. Wendy and I were the first residents to live in the newly decorated flats in Botany Bay, and it was quite the contrast to our rooms at Halls. It felt magical to be able to knock on the door of Front Arch and be let into campus after midnight. We'd take off our heels, and walk over the cobbles, often stopping to sit on the steps leading to the dining hall. It was never something I took for granted, even when I had to dash across Front Square in the pouring rain!

The only negative point about living on campus was how easily distracted you could get from studying. Yes, I was closer to the library, but I was also closer to countless coffeeshops, cinemas and bars. I spent so many afternoons sitting in the Screen cinema by myself when I should have been researching for an essay, meaning that I then had to work all night to reach a deadline. I'd also get phone calls from friends who were over in Doyle's, encouraging me to open my window because they were playing some great tunes. Inevitably, I'd stop what I was doing and go over to join them, drinking cheap vodka with a dash of lime and soda and dancing to the early hours.

Two big changes took place during my time at Trinity, the first being the technological revolution. Though I had a mobile, I still relied on the phone box in halls and then the landline in the flat in Rathmines to call home during the first few years. I would write letters to friends in different universities in Wales and England, and, though I had an email account, I rarely checked it until my time as a Students' Union officer. My First and Second Year essays were handwritten, before we then started using the computer room on-campus to type up and print essays. It was also a time before Facebook and Instagram, and when we still used film in cameras. Luckily, this means that many of my less refined moments are blurry memories or printed photographs rather than available online – something which I'm extremely grateful of!

The second change was the Irish economy. My time in Dublin coincided with the height of the Celtic Tiger and massive expansion across the city. Though I'd been brought up in a household that was quite comfortable financially, it was clear that many of my fellow students came from extremely wealthy families. Whilst I had attended a state school, the majority of those around me had been through private education, and many lived in gorgeous apartments owned by their parents. Not that they flaunted their wealth, but there was a very clear divide between students that had come through the Trinity Access Programme and those who had come straight from school. As my accent gave no clue as to my own background, I was accepted by both groups. I had friends who were mature students that had to work incredibly hard and fight for a place at Trinity, as well as those who had access to money on tap, and were generous with it. It was a genuine eye opener in terms of the wider economic divide.

As Wales was still part of the EU at the time, I was treated the same as Irish students and only required to pay the annual registration fee. However, despite the economic success of Ireland, free university education was still a hotly debated subject and a key focus for many Students' Union demonstrations and campaigns. We sat on O'Connell Bridge and stopped the traffic, and managed to occupy the Department of Education, handcuffing ourselves to radiators. We secured meetings with the Provost and the Ministers for Education, Noel Dempsey and then Mary Hanafin, and were able to secure support for its retention. However, the registration fee to this day continues to rise, and it saddens me to think that people are being costed out of education.

They say that time flies when you're having fun, and certainly my time at Trinity seemed to go by in an instant. The friendships I made remain to this day, and, though we are all now living in different parts of the world, we still keep in touch and share memories via WhatsApp. Every now and then, more pictures are found, and we have great fun trying to figure out when they were taken, who some random boy was in the photo and reminiscing about our student days and activism.

Trinity helped us transition into adults, but we also helped one another. It wasn't just a university. It was a community. And one I'm grateful that I had the opportunity to be a part of.

Heledd Fychan (TCD 1999–2003; History and Political Science) was elected to the Senedd (Welsh Parliament) to represent South Wales Central in May 2021. Prior to this, Heledd worked at the National Museum Wales in Cardiff where she was Head of Policy and Public Affairs. She served on the Board of the UK-wide Museums Association and chaired its Ethics and Nations Committees. Since 2017, she has also been a County Councillor, representing Pontypridd on Rhondda Cynon Taf Council.

FROM RUSSIA WITH LOVE

carl whyte

'**I WANT** to meet some students,' called Pavel Palazhchenko, Mikhail Gorbachev's long-standing interpreter, rather loudly across the Exam Hall. The honorary degree service had finished, and Gorbachev himself stood beside Palazhchenko, drinking from a tiny cup and saucer. It was 8 January 2002, and the last Soviet leader, former General Secretary of the Communist party of the Soviet Union and Nobel Peace Prize Winner, was here in Trinity to receive his Honorary Doctor in Laws (LLD).

I had been told that Students' Union officers, some Russian Language and Politics students and the *Trinity News* writers had been invited, but I couldn't see any other actual students apart from us. I had initially been refused a pass from College for the event. Thankfully Joan, who managed the academic registry office, kindly gave us two tickets so our photographer and I could attend. One of the first things I'd noticed when I arrived was that there were hardly any students in the full-to-capacity Exam Hall.

'Are there any Russian-speaking students?' Pavel continued, on behalf of his boss. My ears pricked up. I spoke some Russian – I'd taken a gap year and lived in Moscow – so I moved towards Dr Gorbachev, our newest graduate, thinking I'd chance my arm with my (very poor) language skills. The Russian students I'd been told were here just didn't seem to materialize

– everyone in the vicinity looked like they'd handed back their library passes a long time ago.

Precisely one minute later, I found myself speaking terrible Russian to the most famous Russian alive. After introductions, I stumbled and Pavel stepped in, simultaneously translating as I reverted to English and we spoke about Dublin, my living in Moscow and the prospect for young Russians of that era.

During commencements, Public Orator John V. Luce had delivered the ceremony in Latin, and afterwards Gorbachev told us, through his translator, that he'd only ever managed to learn one phrase in Latin. So here in Trinity, this colossus of the world stage, a man who had negotiated the START agreement with Ronald Reagan to end the nuclear arms race had sat through his graduation speech without a notion of what was being said about him. And now the first 'Russian-speaking' student he'd been introduced to – me – was blabbering away in Russian about my hobbies and where I went on my holidays! I was about to ask Lenin's successor directions to the train station until, luckily, Pavel the translator staged my rescue.

For me, the whole ceremony summed up perfectly what was right and what was wrong about Trinity. Its global reputation and historical location mean that people like Mikhail Gorbachev are delighted to come to visit and receive honorary degrees. Nelson Mandela had come in the year 2000. But for most students these invite-only events were firmly off-limits – you had no chance of meeting these world leaders or even hearing what they said. The attitude that prevailed was 'little students should be seen and not heard'. Not that I cared back then: I'd gotten an 'interview', we'd gotten some great photographs and it was the front-page story in the next *Trinity News*.

Three years earlier, when I arrived in Trinity, things seemed quite different. I was born and grew up in Belfast (with a stint in south Co. Derry as the Troubles in Belfast raged in the early 1990s), and we'd spent weekends in Dublin since we were young children thanks to the friendship my family had with radio presenter Joe Duffy. My father had been involved in student politics in University of Ulster, and Joe and his wife June had been similarly involved in Trinity. We had visited the campus many times, and I think I had a sense from a young age that this was where I wanted to study. My sister Lara, a couple of years behind me in school, also came to Trinity – she was a junior freshman when I was a senior sophister, the only time in our lives when we were at the same educational institution.

I'd just finished a gap year – I'd travelled to Hungary, Russia and the United States, and was frankly delighted to be back in education. The chaos of those first couple of months always sticks with me, though – unlike my classmates from school who'd gone to UK universities and who had student halls provided, we were just left to fend for ourselves. Trinity Hall had eighty or so rooms at the time, so they were all snapped up and on-campus accommodation was impossible. After a couple of weeks living with Joe and his family – something I'm forever grateful for – I bought a copy of *The Herald* and started looking. I found a place on North Great George's Street and took it all from there.

To start, for us Northerners, much of Trinity is familiar. When I read about how it's seen as a 'Protestant bastion' or 'British bastion', I always think to myself how portraits of royalty or British insignia on public buildings are nothing new when you've grown up in Belfast. Drive to our part of Ireland and all of that is, or was, very familiar. Belfast City Hall, where I spend a lot of time now, is full of paintings of British royalty. Tom Mitchell was Provost when I started at Trinity – the first Catholic to hold the post. Catholics holding senior positions for the first time ever was another thing we were all too familiar with in Belfast.

What I didn't expect, and I'd never imagined was a feeling – in the Freshman year anyway – was that you didn't or couldn't fit in. I studied BESS, and I was struck from very early on how quickly some people seemed to have formed groups and made close friends, and how they certainly weren't looking for any further applicants. After a couple of weeks, the penny dropped that these groups were just groups of school friends, mainly from private schools – institutions we don't have in Northern Ireland – who had just moved on to the same class in Trinity.

It was probably a mixture of inverse snobbery and downright intimidation that meant we kept our distance. I made a lot of friends during my time in Trinity, but either by accident or by circumstance very few came from Dublin. As a fellow Northern classmate expertly phrased it, when it came to Northerners, those from the posh schools 'don't know what box to put us in, so they just don't bother'. That was Trinity, lots of boxes, so it was just a matter of finding which one you belonged to.

My box became *Trinity News* and the Publications Office. Which takes me back to Joe Duffy. Towards the end of my first year, the RTÉ presenter had requested to film on campus for some project and College authorities had flatly refused. The story was that because of his activism as Students' Union President, a deep and everlasting grudge was still held. I'd a sense it was something *Trinity News* might report on, and I knew Joe, so I knocked on the door of the Publications Office in House 6 and introduced myself to the editor, Eoghan Williams, saying I could write about it. That was my start, and I became Assistant Editor in my senior freshman year and Editor in my junior sophister year.

To begin with, I could barely write. By the end of my time at Trinity, I could write a little better, but somehow I had managed to freelance for *Magill Magazine*, the *Sunday World*, the *Sunday Independent* and even had an 'additional reporting' byline in *The Observer*. Thanks to Quark Xpress skills passed down from previous inhabitants of House 6, I had also worked as a subeditor with shifts in newspapers in Belfast at a time when the main daily newspapers were switching en masse to this new design technology. I didn't realize it then, but these were outstanding opportunities at the time, which most universities which had actual courses in journalism couldn't offer.

I had never had a strong inclination to go into journalism, but the politics – or political debate – I saw at the Hist and the Phil just didn't interest me. As far as I was concerned, they were from another planet. My school, St Malachy's College, is the oldest Catholic school in Ulster, and, while we 'debated', the idea of dressing up in black-tie and gowns to stand in a musty old hall just seemed nonsensical, especially at the age of nineteen. As I saw it in Trinity, there was a lot of political debate, but little actual politics. Only when my sister arrived, and became involved in One World Society and the JCR, did I fully appreciate the activism that was going on right across the university.

Trinity News, however, was full of energy, excitement, talent, ability and probably people who wanted to feel some sense of belonging. There were lots of ups and downs. The relationship between College and Publications had always been fraught. I remember being shocked after asking a senior College administrator some rather blithe question, and he barked back at me, 'You'd better get this right or we'll sue you.' I was no legal expert but managed to mumble something about the idiocy of a university suing one of its own students. With hindsight, it was an absolutely unacceptable threat for someone in such a senior position to make to a student, but back then we just shrugged and wrote the story. Staff had previously and successfully sued the student newspaper, so I learned about libel law and all its pitfalls at a very young age.

As a group of students, we were devoted to producing a full broadsheet newspaper covering all aspects of news, arts and sport in the College, and with barely a penny to fund it. If we weren't planning our next edition, we were furiously selling advertising to pay for print costs. We tried to break good stories, learning from some great writers who'd gone just before us – and, looking back, we were threatened with legal action more than we should have been. Eoghan Williams had been a great editor, and I remember Amy Iggulden, who became Features Editor at *The Mail*, doing a report from war-torn Kosovo for *Trinity News*. There was no doubt then that the newspaper had blazed a trail for student journalism across Ireland. Looking back, though, if I knew then what I know now, I'd have scrapped the broadsheet and turned it tabloid, with a bigger focus on the real student stories and sport. Far too much of our time was spent chasing money and advertising.

Books like *Tender* and *Normal People* I think tell the truth about Trinity, but we were so caught up in producing the actual newspaper that I'm not sure a lot of what we wrote stands the test of time. That was my fault; the writers themselves were generally brilliant. Many involved went on to top positions in journalism: Kate Devlin became Chief Political Correspondent at *The Times*, and Susan Thompson became Business Correspondent at the same newspaper. Gerard Cowan wrote for the *Wall Street Journal*. Photographer Phoebe Ling's work has appeared in *The New York Times* and the National Portrait Gallery. Tim Walker, Music Editor, who edited the Trinity Ball Guide, has written for *The Independent* and *The Guardian* ever since. I'm glad that during our time Trinity continued its tradition of producing some of the country's best journalists, without having a single course in journalism, and largely unknown and unacknowledged by the university itself.

As for academic study, I managed to get it together in my final year, and by some miracle grabbed a First. BESS is a completely overwhelming course in First and Second Year: lectures with hundreds of students combined with tutorials with completely disinterested teaching assistants mean that it is far from the romantic picture painted in the prospectus. Things changed though in the sophister years. I did Economics and Business Studies, and lecturers like Mary Keating, Martin King and Gemma Donnelly-Cox were outstanding in their ability to get the best from those they taught. With the exception of Professors P.J. Drudy and John O'Hagan, most Economics lecturers just passed me by – too many students, subjects that were too complex to get into detail on and a feeling sometimes from staff that they just didn't have to bother about students. More than likely it was my own lack of interest, or my focus on *Trinity News*.

My graduation was in December 2003, but years later I still have a copy of the proclamation made by Professor Luce during Gorbachev's ceremony. I find the last paragraph strangely beautiful because it sums up what Trinity at least tried to do for all of us. Talking about the former Soviet leader, and addressing the assembled guests at the end of the oration, Luce proclaimed:

'He comes as a most welcome guest to our College, where free investigation and the love of learning have flourished for upwards of four hundred years. We salute in him an honourable patriot, and a humane and magnanimous citizen of the world.

'Let us enrol him in our society with your warmest applause ringing in his ears.'

That warmest applause, for those of us anointed with a Trinity degree, is the one common experience we all share. Nearly every single one of us has stood on that stage in the Exam Hall, listening to applause, which rings in our ears for many years to come, as we take the lessons of our time there – lessons learned through labour and through love, forward into the rest of our lives.

Carl Whyte (TCD 1999–2003; Economics and Business Studies) is currently the Social Democratic and Labour Party's Political and Policy Director. In May 2019 he was elected to represent the area he grew up in as a Belfast City Councillor. Since graduating from Trinity, he has completed postgraduates in International Relations at Johns Hopkins University and in Law at Queen's University Belfast. His daughter Stephanie is four years old and has already visited Trinity twice!

'EDUCATE YOURSELF THAT YOU MAY BE FREE'

paul o'connell

'... so I say to you all
To educate yourself, become well read
And start to use the head, contemplate your own situation
Find the true enemy and stop banging heads
With the victims of its greed.'
—Damien Dempsey

MY FIRST clear memory of Trinity College is from around 1995. I was fourteen, had been suspended from school indefinitely, and me and a group of friends 'bonked' the DART into town to go on a ramble. After being chased out of shops on Grafton Street, and causing a nuisance around Stephen's Green, we made our way to the front entrance of Trinity on Dame Street and into Front Square of Trinity College. I remember, still, being struck by the otherworldly character of the place – the cobbled yard, the columns on either side and the Campanile. Nobody from Kilbarrack, or at least nobody we knew, had gone to college or university, and certainly not to Trinity. It felt very much like sneaking into somewhere you didn't belong, a feeling reinforced by the security guards shadowing us. I still remember that I thought the Front Square *was* Trinity.

It was only years later, when I got a place on the first Trinity Access Programme (TAP) foundation course for young adults in 1999, that I learned of the full dimensions of the Trinity campus and began to get a sense of life in this university. Those of us on the foundation course were based just outside the walls of the main campus – symbolic, perhaps – in a building beside Pearse Street train station.

The new foundation course offered students who had not secured the requisite Leaving Cert points for the course they wanted to study at Trinity a bridging year to support them in pursuing a degree at the university. During this year, students took a number of introductory courses, either in arts and humanities, social sciences or the hard sciences, alongside general study skills classes. If you successfully completed the year, you could then interview for a place on your preferred undergraduate course, with a number of places reserved in each course for TAP students.

I remember that, as part of my foundation year, TAP staff organized mock interviews for us to get ready for the real thing. When it was my turn one of the interviewers, who had been brought in for the exercise, asked me: 'What would you say to people who say the Access Program is a back door into Trinity?' I replied, off the cuff, 'I'd say they're right, but it's a back door that's needed because the front door isn't open to everyone.' I think at the time I might have felt a bit defensive or offended by this question. But also, as the person who asked it was a Trinity graduate with a David Norris accent, it just reinforced for me how much class conditions how people see and live in this world.

It's more than twenty years since that interview, and while those in TAP, and other access programmes around the country, have done immense work in that time, inequality in access to higher education in Ireland remains deeply entrenched. This is something I was aware of going into Trinity. When I was fourteen, I was kicked out of school – the straw that broke the camel's back was when I broke an older students' nose in a fight, but me being kicked out had been on the cards for some time.

My two older brothers had also been kicked out of school, and in an area with high levels of deprivation and poverty, early school leaving was and remains all too common. So, when I went to school, I always expected to be kicked out – I always expected to go to prison too (pretty much every male in my family and extended family has been locked up at one time or another), but thankfully I've managed to avoid that.

While I was out of school, I gained a degree of political awareness so that when I was allowed back into school (on the eve of my Junior Cert) I had already started developing clear ideas about the role of class in society, and the inequality and injustice produced by it. There were a number of factors that spurred this bourgeoning awareness and interest in learning and ideas. My father – who left school at eleven and was locked up for a crime he didn't commit when he was seventeen – would regularly talk to me about how the system was stacked against us, and how we had to be smart to not get chewed up by it. I also read a lot of Irish history around this time, and Thomas Davis's injunction to 'educate that you may be free' resonated.

My time at Trinity reinforced that. The Access Programme was a great step, but the fact that we were based physically outside the walls of Trinity perhaps reinforced that those of us from working-class backgrounds (or deprived communities) could be allowed *in* Trinity but were not part *of* it. This suited me, as I went in there with a strong attitude of reverse class-snobbery. I would attend my classes, but then get out as quickly as I could to be with 'my people'. This is not to say I did not get on with other students on my course or in Trinity. I met some great people, but normally they'd be from outside Dublin, mature or international students. Too many of the others seemed like genuine fodder for a Ross O'Carroll-Kelly column, and I had no interest in engaging with them.

It was, in hindsight, a strange and dislocating experience to go from an afternoon seminar on Gramsci, or later on vicarious liability, to an evening at the Black Sheep in Coolock, or The Harp at O'Connell Bridge, and ending the night in a fight over some nonsense. I'd sleep it off over the weekend, and then I was back into Trinity for a discussion on Freire's pedagogy, or John Kelly's views on reforming the Irish Constitution.

But, for me, it worked. I had returned to secondary school after my suspension with a passion for learning and went into Trinity with the intention of studying English and History, to then go on and become a secondary-school teacher. This was important for me, as I understood that the efforts some of my teachers (in particular Fionnuala Walsh, Moira Glackin and, at an earlier point in time, Dick Fields) had made to help and support me made a huge difference in my life, and I wanted to do the same.

The year I spent on the foundation course (1999–2000) was fantastic. We were introduced to a range of subjects. (I recall writing an essay comparing Shakespeare to the Wu-Tang Clan, and another on Gramsci.) The staff at TAP (Cliona, Kathleen, Sheila, Elaine and others) were brilliant: friendly, supportive and genuinely committed to helping people from working-class areas pursue further education. There was a great group of students on the course too.

During my time with TAP, one of the staff on the course suggested that because of my 'argumentative streak' I should think about studying Law. The thought hadn't crossed my mind previously: growing up in Kilbarrack, my main experience of 'the law' had been the unchecked brutality working-class people, including my family and neighbours, were subjected to by gardaí on a regular basis. We received a very clear message that the law was something we were subject to; it was not something to protect or support us.

Prompted by this suggestion, I picked up a copy of a recently published book: *Crime and Poverty in Ireland* (1998). I discovered that somewhere in the region of 50 per cent of the prisoners in Mountjoy Prison came from five working-class areas around Dublin, areas like Kilbarrack. At the same time, there was another report about how a strikingly high number of entrants into Trinity came from a handful of private schools. This contrast struck me at the time, and in a vague and general way I thought that if I studied Law, I could become a solicitor and use the law to make a difference for working-class communities.

I was interviewed for, and offered a place, in Law by Professor Yvonne Scannell and went on to study for my LLB at Trinity from 2000–4. I remember in one of my first tutorials, on criminal law, having a very different take on the law from my classmates from the outset. One of the first questions was 'what is a crime?' – to which the textbook answer is 'anything that causes moral or physical harm'. Having seen how working-class communities were disproportionately and systematically punished, while the 'cute hoors' that peopled the Moriarty and other tribunals got away scot-free with much more serious transgressions, my response was that the law had to be understood, first and foremost, as a mechanism of class control.

I've refined that assessment a little over the years, but the central premise that informed my approach to law in that early tutorial was only reinforced throughout my time studying the law at Trinity, and in my subsequent studies and political activism. Trinity Law School had some of the foremost experts on various aspects of law in Ireland, and it was a pleasure to be taught by William Binchy, Ivana Bacik, Gerry Whyte, Neville Cox and others. I remember to this day the thrill of first walking through the Berkeley Library, the rooms stacked floor to ceiling with books.

I was entranced by the smell of books, a funny habit I still have now when I explore secondhand bookshops. There's an old hardback copy of *Albion's Fatal Tree* somewhere in Trinity, and I remember it being one of the most beautiful things I'd seen. It was also a book that first made me think seriously about the ideological role of law in society, and very much shaped how I came to view law in general – with thanks to Ivana Bacik's class on Criminology, for introducing me to it.

The 1913 Reading Room struck me as the very epitome of what a university and 'learning' was – I spent hours in there, reading for my course and whatever else captured my interest. Nowadays, I teach Law in a university in London. Because everything is digitized these days, I really feel my students miss out on the experience of wandering the shelves of law reports, finding the one they are looking for and then reading through it, accompanied by the marginal notes of the generations of law students that went before them.

On the other hand, I also remember the strange discovery that some students would pull pages out of law reports, or other books, after they had read them. Presumably this was the competitive edge cultivated in fee-paying schools, or by the destructive pressure of the Leaving Cert's zero-sum ethic. Either way, it struck me as both bizarre and profoundly sad, that people who had every advantage and privilege would feel the need, out of a sense of being in competition with everyone around them, to vandalize a book.

The sense of being in Trinity but not of it is something that every working-class person that goes in there knows. In the second or third year of my Law degree I was in the Buttery for lunch and passed a table with a group of builders sat at it when one of them called my name. It was Philly, a friend I'd hung out with a lot when I was out of school. During that time, me, him and our group of friends did all the things that young people out of school in deprived communities the world over do – petty crime, more violence than I care to recall and all manner of other nonsense.

I hunkered down at the edge of the table, exchanged a few words – 'How's things? What's such and such up to? Locked up? Has a kid now!' – the usual. One of Philly's co-workers – they must have been doing scaffolding on campus – turned to him and said, 'How the fuck do you know somebody in Trinity?' To which Philly replied, with a wry wink, 'He wasn't always in Trinity.' This exchange again reinforced for me that sense of Trinity as a place that people like me didn't quite belong in – how could someone from Kilbarrack know somebody in Trinity, let alone be in Trinity?

There were, indeed, a half-dozen times when I nearly left, especially in the first year or two. The work was fine and interesting, but all my friends had taken up apprenticeships or other jobs. Meanwhile, I'd spend most Friday afternoons heading to the ATM at Pearse Street station, as it was one of the few that dispensed £5 notes. I just wanted to have something in my pocket. I found that side of it hard, and that was with a grant, support from TAP and no fees. I can't even imagine how working-class students find it possible to pursue higher education now, given the increased marketization of the sector and punitive cost of living in Dublin, and indeed throughout Ireland.

Before going to Trinity, I had been politically active for a few years, but never got involved with the politics on-campus. Like much else there, it just seemed divorced from my reality – in Kilbarrack we were dealing with the scourge of heroin, problems of poverty, unemployment and deprivation. I was still developing my own political analysis, so out of curiosity went to a seminar organized by a student society on campus. At it, some of the most comically posh young people I'd ever encountered sat around discussing alienation, what the working class was, what it needed, wanted and so on. I left halfway through. I don't doubt their sincerity, but it was laughable, and a little dispiriting, to see such important ideas and issues being discussed by people who, beyond the theoretical, really had no understanding of them. Unfortunately, this mildly irritating student radicalism is something I have seen time and again over the years. It only reinforces for me the need for working-class people – those with a real need for and claim to the ideas of socialism – to develop their own institutions of education.

In early 2013, I was invited back to Trinity to mark the twentieth anniversary of TAP. At the time, I was teaching at the University of Leicester and was just about to head off to Harvard for a year as a visiting fellow. At the event, I gave a brief speech reflecting on my own experiences of TAP and on a report TAP had commissioned for the occasion. One of the key findings of this report was that working-class people who had gone through higher education often experienced severe and difficult dislocation. Not quite being part of the new scene, but then also being somewhat set apart in the areas and communities they came from. This is certainly something I felt while in Trinity and still do today.

I'd been asked to speak at the event as an example of the success of access programmes, and I was happy to do this. But I also made the point, with the then Minister for Education sat beside me, that any success I may have achieved was also an indictment of the inequalities in Irish society and the education system. Tens of thousands of people more capable than me are systematically denied the possibility to develop themselves, to reach their potential and experience the benefits of education – my time at Trinity, and my working life since then, has taught me that time and again.

In writing these reflections now, I find it hard to believe that it was twenty-two years ago when I started on the foundation course. I didn't become a secondary-school teacher, as originally planned, but have become an educator – for almost seventeen years I've taught Law at universities in Ireland and Britain. My time in Trinity prepared me well for the intellectual rigour my work requires, and coming at it through the TAP year and from a 'non-traditional' background (in the palatable jargon of funders and sociologists) has shaped how I approach my own teaching and research.

I make it my business to support all my students, but in particular those from working-class backgrounds. In my research and political activism, I continue to work, in whatever way I can, to try and build a society where something like the access programme will not be needed – where it will be viewed as the quaint necessity of a less evolved period. A society in which an institution with the resources and history of Trinity is at the service of all, without the need for back doors.

Dr Paul O'Connell (TCD 1999–2000, Trinity Access Programme Foundation Year; 2000–4 Law) is from Kilbarrack in Dublin and was the first in his family to go to university. After completing his studies at Trinity, he went on to secure an LLM and PhD in Law from the National University of Ireland, Galway. Paul has taught Law at universities in Ireland and Britain since 2005, and publishes on human rights, public law and Marxist approaches to law. Paul is currently Reader in Law at SOAS University of London.

ONE WORLD ON CAMPUS

khalid ibrahim

WHEN I first set foot in Trinity College Dublin in 1998, I felt like I belonged again to life. There were so many beautiful things that deepened my attachment and love for Trinity. I used to go into College early in the mornings to see tourists from all over the world fill Front Square, and I would watch them listening attentively to many details about its ancient history and taking pictures in every corner of its campus. Trinity is renowned for its reputation in distinguished scientific research; it is also responsible for an instant feeling of renewable energy and the feeling that you are *living* life, while groups of people and students fill all the spaces around you with their noise, discussions and play.

Even when you wanted to go outside of College, you would see another more vocal life surrounding it – like a bracelet on your wrist – in College Green, Grafton Street and O'Connell Street. I felt the depth and joy of these moments inside and outside Trinity. I felt suffocated when I visited other universities to participate in student activities, as though I was in a barren desert.

I am an Iraqi from a kingdom of fear and oppression. In Iraq there was one party: the party of the dictator Saddam. Saddam, whose pictures in millions were twice the number of the population and had to be placed in every home and office. Whenever he visited an area, Saddam was accompanied by a full military division. To approach him and shake hands with him would have been a dream. I remember one of my acquaintances whose car stopped in the street leading to the Republican Palace almost got into a big problem with the guards. In Iraq during that time, you were a criminal even before you knew the accusation, and you were a member of their party even if you did not want to belong to it. Dissenting opinions were not respected. Other opinions meant death or imprisonment, torture and the loss of everything.

Trinity was far from Iraq, where Saddam's dictatorship suppressed public freedoms – in particular, freedom of opinion. In contrast, education in Trinity was not indoctrination. During Freshers' Week, politicians – including the Taoiseach – arrived without guards or processions to meet student party members and discuss the country's general policy. In Trinity's classes there was a lot of room for creativity and scholarly debate, and I also found most of my colleagues picked subjects that they really had a desire to study. Trinity gave great incentives to outstanding students. In many cases, I evaluated the work my colleagues had done while they evaluated my work in a transparent academic atmosphere and in the presence of the teaching staff. This practice enriched and encouraged scientific research. Students were generally self-confident, and mostly lived independently of their families on campus or somewhere in Dublin 6.

The relationship between teachers and students was constructive, and the professors were understanding and ready to help students face their responsibilities in any way possible. Many lecturers became friends of mine whom I still keep in touch with every now and then.

I liked that a number of my fellow students became the leading politicians in the country soon after their graduation, including Averil Power and Lucinda Creighton. The opportunity was always available for everyone to create their own future. I was an eyewitness to a great confrontation that took place between Power and Creighton in 2002 over the abortion referendum. Averil led the Students' Union's neutral stance, and Lucinda led the Trinity Abortion Referendum Taskforce (TART), which was a pro-choice group at the time. She changed her views on abortion in the years afterwards. The 2002 referendum failed, and both succeeded in their political life. Both resigned from their original parties: Averil became a senator and Lucinda a TD from 2007 to 2016.

The TCD campus contained all the essentials for students, with libraries everywhere as well as computer rooms, restaurants and a whole building for sports. If you suffered from mental-health problems, you could access the counselling services in addition to a well-equipped health centre. During one of my school years, I suffered from a severe cold, so I went to the centre where the receptionist asked me whether I had made an appointment in advance. I told her I had not, but that I was in bad health and needed treatment, and I waited for hours. I left the clinic without treatment, and after that I wrote a letter which was published in the Students' Union newspaper, the *University Record*. Then the director of the health centre called me and we discussed the issue, and the director became my own GP and a friend to whom I talked a lot about Iraq.

My life at Trinity was complemented by the One World Society. It was one of the most successful societies in TCD, and even won the title of Best Society many times. Over the years, we had members from many countries, all united in defending human rights and the cultures of peoples in the developing world.

Freshers' Week dazzled me with its efficiency and democratic atmosphere (that first year and in all the years following). My link with the One World Society began in Freshers' Week in 1998. I was in Front Square, checking out the student societies' stands. I registered myself as a member without hesitation and paid the subscription fee, which was one Irish pound. At the time, I never could have imagined that I would become its coordinator for many of the following years and a successful chairperson for one of those years.

One World Society's annual Multiculturalism Week was first opened in 1998 by the then Provost Dr Thomas T. Mitchell. This week included a food festival as one of its central activities. We sourced food from twenty countries, although all the food was consumed even before the festival started. A flood of about 400 students found their way into the GMB, a small hall supposed to cater for only about 150 students. In 1999, twenty-two countries were represented, and the food was available for only fifteen minutes after the door opened. After this, we moved to the dining hall where there is a capacity for 400 students, but again we exceeded this number. In 2000, we sourced food from twenty-five countries and there was enough for every single participant. I think it was one of the most popular student events at the time.

There were many other activities in addition to Multiculturalism Week. During the era of Saddam Hussein, the One World Society also organized several events highlighting Iraq, including several annual Iraqi weeks with a variety of cultural activities, in addition to other cultural nights, such as Inuit night, Scottish night, Japanese night and other events. We worked tirelessly – as volunteers – day and night. We supported Palestine, and from our room in House 6 we organized the largest pro-Palestine demonstration in Dublin.

Diver(c)ity Magazine was born in the womb of the One World Society, and its first issue was published in October 1999, featuring a number of topics concerned with human rights and multiculturalism. The magazine continued to grow until its fourth issue, when it was taken over by DU Publications. It ceased publishing in 2004. At the beginning of its publication, I was part of the editorial staff, during which time I wrote a number of articles and supervised the printing of the first four issues. It was the first magazine to specialize in multiculturalism since Trinity's foundation in 1592.

In July 2001, members of the One World Society travelled across Europe to participate in the anti-globalization demonstration outside the G8 Summit in Genoa. I decided to go with them. Our car drove through Britain, France, Monte Carlo and then Italy. It was a very enjoyable trip, and in Genoa we camped in small tents. On the appointed day – 20 July 2001 – we happily joined the big demonstration. We did not know what fate would be waiting for us. The next day, the Italian police attacked us with batons and tear-gas canisters, and a left-wing group clashed with the police after they killed an Italian demonstrator named Carlo Giuliani. The next day, we were all out in thousands denouncing the murder. Demonstrations had now become a tool for us, so when we returned we did not go home but instead organized a silent sit-in to protest in front of the Italian embassy in Dublin.

They were unforgettable, delicious days, full of happiness and success. I met many loyal friends, three of whom headed the society while I continued to be a coordinator. Vanessa was doing a PhD while chairing the group; Philip's period of presidency was marked by many successful activities. Under his leadership, the group was awarded Best Medium Society at the Central Societies Committee Awards. Incidentally, I told him one day that he should marry Julia and encouraged him to do so. This is indeed what happened, and they are happy now with four joyful children.

Iraq was with me my whole time in TCD. In the mid-90s and upon arrival in Ireland, I established the Iraqi Human Rights Organisation in Ireland with some Iraqi colleagues. As I joined TCD in 1998, its real HQ was in House 6 as well. We organized a lot of anti-Saddam demonstrations, and we used to stand just opposite the college in front of the Bank of Ireland every Sunday demanding his removal and an end to sanctions. We used to store all our materials in College.

I celebrated the removal of Saddam in College with my friends. It felt like it was the right time to go back to Iraq, but it took me a further eight years to leave Dublin and return to Baghdad.

I loved many aspects of my time in Trinity. It meant a lot to be based in the heart of the city, and to be no more than a short walk away from the real life of people and everything else that Dublin may offer. I came here from Iraq, a country in which people were killed just for expressing their views publicly. In Trinity, I could witness students from the two Trinity debating societies (the Phil and the Hist) debating freely with politicians on all the important issues. It felt fantastic.

There is a wish in the depth of my heart. It is to return to Trinity to revive the One World Society, which was dissolved in 2007. I hope – as agreed with my friend Philip, who is doing an MSc in the College right now – to participate in the next Freshers' Week, promoting the work of the One World Society, promoting its focus on defending people's rights in the developing world and supporting multiculturalism.

Khalid Ibrahim (TCD 1998–2006; MSc/PhD Health Informatics) is an Iraqi with decades of experience in the human rights field, including more than ten years on the Dublin staff of the Frontline Defenders. Khalid studied Health Informatics for his MSc in TCD. He continued on to take a PhD in the use of new technologies to enhance human rights protection in the Middle East and North Africa, but moved to Beirut before the completion of his thesis. Khalid is the Executive Director of the Gulf Centre for Human Rights. He is currently moving between Beirut and his hometown of Baghdad.

HINDSIGHT

elske rahill

1. ARTS BLOCK

I don't know what I expected university to look like, but it didn't match the ugly concrete structure of Trinity's less-celebrated Nassau Street side.

It's only on writing this piece that I googled the history of the Arts Building – or 'Arts Block' as it is colloquially known – and was disabused of the idea that the building was brand new when I arrived in 2000. I now realize how ludicrously ignorant that notion was. As it turns out, the Arts Block was completed in 1978, before I was even born, and anyone looking at it could guess as much.

My excuse is that somehow the characterlessness of the place gave it a kind of ahistoricism for me. The rooms, the lecture halls, the corridors all had a hush of neutrality about them – everything was either beige or grey or brown. And, in fairness, it smelled like a new building: fish glue and photocopiers and something synthetically clean. Coupled with the constant muttering from lecturers about the ugliness of the rooms and the lack of natural light, this gave me the lasting and until-now unchallenged impression that it had only just been built.

Entering Trinity from Nassau Street, you can either go straight onto Main Square via 'The Ramp' – a short, paved slope leading down to the cobblestones (always bottlenecked by loitering students) – or turn right into an indoor space giving onto lecture halls, a series of boxed-off stairwells and an entrance to the library. This is the Arts Block. There are swing doors into these stairwells, opening to squeaky steps running from the ground floor up through the various Arts departments.

The English department was on the fourth floor. To me, every floor looked the same, and every corridor off every floor looked the same. At first, I got lost a lot.

2. BAD ATTITUDE

My Fresher year is a misty and somewhat patchy memory. Even at the time it was all a bit of a haze. I wish I was citing a haze of partying and intellectual fervour, sex and drugs, but it was none of those things. I was agonizingly self-conscious and terribly lonely, and I think it's safe to say I 'failed to engage', so my account is probably lacking some basics, like the names of lecturers or the popular academic ideas of the time ... but this is what I do remember:

To me, the other students seemed predominantly American or English. This is probably because they were more visible and audible than native students. They had loud voices, accents that demanded an audience and the kind of confidence that takes generations to engender. The girls – and they were mostly girls – had names like Carmen, Beatrice and Daphne. They wore expensive fabrics and seemed to have scarves everywhere – on their heads, around their necks and shoulders and sometimes their hips – and these scarves seemed to get flipped and draped and swung around a lot. They took up a lot of space. The boys wore Byronic shirts and Byronic hair, floppy shoes and jumpers that had been designed with elbow patches. They had names like Orlando.

3. UNTEACHABLE

I wrote my first essay in pencil on the bus on the day it was due. I was given a first for it, and took this to mean that I was really very clever and wouldn't, or shouldn't, have to make any effort at university.

It is fair to say that, for the first two years at least, I did not take advantage of the opportunity afforded me. I read the core texts and winged my way through exams and essays based on my own interpretation, as though reading secondary texts was a kind of cheating that was beneath me.

Of course, it was the arrogance of the desperately insecure. The Arts Block would bring on a kind of panic in me. If I tried to speak in class, my voice stuck in my throat or I said things I didn't even mean. I felt intimidated and frustrated. I missed a lot of lectures simply because I couldn't face leaving my room.

We received compulsory tutorials in Critical and Cultural Theory from a man with a broad, smooth head and a slow, smooth voice, who commanded a kind of giddy awe from the other students. I honestly don't know his name, but I think he must have been a big deal. Out of pure counter-suggestiveness, I hated him, and out of pure terror, I hated the subject.

Our core text was a big tome of writings on structuralism, postmodernism and so on. It had a picture of a corpse being dissected on the cover and contained a lot of ideas I had never come across before. They completely bamboozled me, and I resisted them tooth and nail. For one thing, I thought of myself as an outsider. I was used to feeling subversive, and so, when an authority figure tried to teach a deeper kind of subversion, I just didn't know what to do. For another, I was still of the belief that art contained transcendent truths independent of political or historical context. Literature meant a lot to me – it was a kind of religion for my eighteen-year-old self – and I felt very threatened by its deconstruction. To me, the Critical and Cultural Theory module seemed bent on robbing everything of meaning.

It was only years later that I would learn to engage with the likes of Lacan, Foucault, Derrida, etc. Back then, I laughed at it all as a kind of useless mental acrobatics that I, as a more authentic being, would have to rise above. One assignment I remember quite vividly was an essay on Structuralism in which I drew a pair of pants, labelled 'pants'. I thought it was brilliant and brave of me, and would have been delighted with either a first or a fail, but instead I received a bored 2.2 from a lecturer who had seen it all before. To my credit, at least I had the awareness to feel embarrassed when I got the essay back.

My favourite class was Greek Theatre. It was poorly subscribed – there were three or four of us in the class – Caitríona Lally, who I became friends with, and some quiet boys from other courses. It was taught by an extremely elderly lecturer in one of the tiny upstairs rooms. He spent a great deal of time quoting the original texts in their original language, which I didn't understand a word of. I enjoyed his classes – his enthusiasm alone was inspiring. He would spittle-roar passages from the plays and, as far as I remember, passionately dismissed the reading (Hegel's?) that ancient Greek society was harmonious. This was the only module I really 'got into'. He assumed we were familiar with all of the suggested readings, and so I was shamed into reading them. These were the first secondary texts I actually engaged with. They were written in the 70s or 80s and could only be found in the library and read *in situ*. The spines were very brittle, and they smelled. I very much enjoyed disagreeing with them.

4. PLAYERS

By the time I arrived at Trinity, I had long assumed that I was going to be a writer – I wrote all the time, I couldn't help it. I had been told from a young age not to expect to earn a living that way, and I had accepted that. Yet, somehow, I was naïve enough to believe that acting was a more viable option. I thought it was the only 'job' I could enjoy or excel at or get paid for. Along with every aspiring teen actor in the country, I had been to a fruitless call-back for *Felicity's Journey* a couple of years before, which I considered a near miss. Then, I had won a part in a short Disney film the summer after my Leaving Cert, bringing in more money than I had ever held in my hand before. The work was thrilling and the money seemed great, and I was quite confident I could make a career of it.

The most important friendships of my adolescence were not made at any of the many schools I had attended, but at a weekly drama class. My 'gang' was a small, eclectic group of middle-class outsiders who had been sent as children to Betty Ann Norton's School of Speech and Drama. Betty Ann was an un-age-able but certainly elderly Northsider who, along with her brother Jim, had been given elocution lessons by a kindly neighbour. She was once an act*or*, but now she taught instead because, she told us in her loud RP, 'There are NO PARTS FOR WOMEN.' She was formidable in every way. She spoke to us like adults. She introduced me not only to literature (she had us reading Joyce and Woolf at age twelve) but to the thrill of not-being-yourself and of being part of something else.

I had auditioned for the Beckett Course – Trinity's prestigious 'vocational' acting course that has since been shut down. When, to my indignity, I was rejected, I was left no choice but to do my first CAO option: a BA in English

Studies. I still thought acting was for me, and made it my mission to get a part in a play. I auditioned for two Players productions: *Everyman*, directed by Alice Coughlin, and *Hamletmachine*, directed by Kate McLoughlin.

I played Good Deeds and Ophelia respectively. In both plays I was naked but for flesh-coloured knickers and some tastefully pinned muslin. I put everything into these roles, rehearsing through classes and learning all my lines before the first rehearsal. The dressing room smelled like poster paint, and everyone there was friendly and passionate. I had a terrible crush on the loinclothed Everyman, and nothing but revulsion for the guy who played Hamlet.

In *Hamletmachine,* I hung from the scaffolding, emerged from a coffin and played alongside two large, silent, naked girls wrapped in clingfilm. Kate wanted her theatre space to be a multisensory experience, so our set featured real rotting meat – a tongue and some organs, falling from the open door of a broken fridge. The theatre stank more and more as the week-long-run progressed. The tongue grew white spores, then blue. I loved every minute.

I was intimidated by the clique who ran Players, though. Even when invited, I shied away from their parties and never involved myself any further than auditioning for roles or directing plays. This is another regret, because every minute I did spend there I loved, and I would later develop friendships with some of the people I spent my first couple of years avoiding.

5. BIG BREAK

In Second Year, family difficulties took over everything, and I engaged even less in college. After being shouted at by one tutor for never turning up for class, I realized I couldn't carry on. I remember going to my tutor – Stephen Matterson – to explain the situation. He was impatient with me, I don't think the situation made any sense to him. (In fairness, it didn't make much sense to me either.)

'What would you like me to do?'

'I'd like a year out.'

'Okay.'

During my year out, I got a job as a receptionist at Trinity Lodge Hotel. I spent the day sitting behind a desk taking bookings, licking stamps, answering the phone and writing the first draft of my first novel, *Between Dog and Wolf*. I left when I landed the title role in Marina Carr's *Ariel* at the Abbey Theatre.

I loved being in the theatre, although when I think of some of the things I said back then, I cringe. I was absolutely affected, naïve and self-centred. Too much so, I think, for a woman of nineteen. It was an impressive cast. Amongst them were the last of the 'Abbey Actors' – actors who were paid lifelong retainers by the national theatre and had to be available for any play they were called to. They included Joan O'Hara, who, at seventy-two, swam in the sea every morning. She is the first person I have ever met to cheerfully declare that she was ready to die. She said this regularly, though I think she went on to live for another decade or so. There was the grouchy Des Cave, who was not happy to be there.

Rehearsals were slightly ridiculous, with Marina Carr refusing to articulate any 'meaning', and the director, Conall Morrison, projecting a political subtext (the Iraq War, I think) that Marina didn't seem to agree with and the actors didn't at all seem to care about, though the younger ones pretended to.

The play was an unmitigated flop. After the run, I struggled to get any acting work, except a 'feature extra' role in *Shaun of the Dead* and, later, a role as a Russian woman (speaking Russian for the first time in my life. I think there was a mix-up, and they thought I was Russian) in *Fair City*.

I spent the summer in Paris with Mary – a friend from Betty Ann's. At €200 for 3 months, we sublet a tiny bedsit on the eleventh floor of an apartment building. The idea was to get jobs and learn French, but after applying for Disneyland, a few Irish bars and some nanny jobs, we realized the only posts we were eligible for were as 'model and muse' for young male painters. It was amazing how many of these advertisements there were, and how close we came to turning up for our interviews.

We ended up busking in St Michel and the Champs-Élysées, playing trad music on a viola (hers) and fiddle (mine). There was a heatwave that summer, and we would busk, sweating through 'I'll Tell Me Ma' and 'Raglan Road', until we had enough for a kebab or a crepe, busk again until we had enough for ice cream and breakfast the next day, then walk home again with our instruments on our backs. I finished the first draft of my book.

6. BEING SOCIABLE

The situation with my family had by now stabilized. I was quickly becoming disillusioned with the whole acting thing. I had read a lot during my 'year out', learned how hopeless I was at waitressing and how much I hated working at a till, and returned to college a little wiser and readier to learn.

I started back in Third Year, working as a lounge girl at O'Neill's pub and as a float for the Dublin branches of Butler's Chocolate Café, of which there were many at that time. I made a conscious decision that this year I would: a) be more sociable and friendlier to my peers, and b) get a boyfriend – I was 20 years old and had never had one.

I got a lot more out of the courses that year. I wrote a play, *After Opium*, and directed it at Players, and then at the Project Arts Centre.

The problem with being sociable is that it was counter-intuitive for me. I had to force myself to accept advances of friendship or romance, and, because I was working against my instinct anyway, I was not as discerning as I should have been.

There were some strange encounters, and I learned that people could be hard to shake. There was a Marxist Indian prince (by his account) who was always stoned, slept on my couch a lot, and had a thing for blue eyes. I'm not even sure if he was enrolled in Trinity. There was also an Erasmus student who auditioned for my play, then asked if I wanted to 'hang out'. We 'hung out' – first at a pub theatre, then my flat, until 3 am, when I asked her to leave. She turned up again an hour later with a backpack of clothes, books and CDs, saying she had fought with her roommate over toothpaste. She slept in my room for over a month, and I really didn't have the wherewithal to make her leave until an acting friend offered to move in 'on top' of her. I learned years later that we were known as a couple, though nothing could have been further from the truth.

As for the boyfriend idea, following my crush on my Players co-star, then my Abbey director, there was simply no one I 'fancied'. Mary and I agreed that this didn't matter – we just needed to be more normal, and have boyfriends, like normal people. I went on a few dates where, out of boredom, I lied elaborately before getting dry-humped in the lobby of my apartment block. I would then tie my lies in with my next-day break-up call.

Eventually, I went out with the most persistent of these. In the last year of my degree, I found out I was pregnant.

7. GROWING UP

I remember the day I took the pregnancy test, breaking down at a dissertation meeting with my supervisor. She was incredibly kind but also – I think this is testament to how different things were then – suggested that having a baby might bring me 'closer' to a boyfriend with whom, to say the least, things 'weren't working'.

My tutor was a man from the Classics department – incredibly gentle and kind, passing on advice about morning sickness from his wife and sorting out all the admin. I was too ill with the pregnancy to sit my finals. I couldn't believe how supportive they were at Trinity about me postponing them until after the baby was born. I even got breastfeeding breaks during my exams.

I had already secured a place on the Creative Writing MPhil course for the following year, and they agreed to hold it for me. By the time I began the course, I was single mother to a nine-month-old baby. I am extremely fortunate, I think, to have had that year to write, and I blush when I think of the liberties I took. Sometimes, for example, I brought my son into class with me, where he would sit very quietly, scribbling on paper, smiling and being passed around the class. I thought everyone was delighted with him.

Elske Rahill with her son, Phoenix, 2006. Photo credit: Felicienne Rahill.

Oddly enough, I think that is the first year I really appreciated the value of being at Trinity, and the first year I really worked hard.

I returned in 2010 to what was then the Gender and Women's Studies department (now absorbed into the English or History department). That is another story, but it brought home the truth of that graduate cliché. Returning, I realized how lucky I had been to have access to that kind of education, and how little I had understood that privilege at the time.

Elske Rahill (TCD 2000–5, English Studies; 2006–7, MPhil Creative Writing and Publishing; 2009–10, PGDip Gender and Women's Studies) is an Irish novelist and short story writer. Her work includes the novels **Between Dog and Wolf** (2013, The Lilliput Press), **An Unravelling** (Head of Zeus and The Lilliput Press, 2019) and the short story collection **In White Ink** (2017). She currently lives in Burgundy, France with her partner and four children.

SHAPESHIFTING

dave ring

FRESHERS' WEEK in 2000, my dad had flown over with me from the States to settle me in. I'd been assigned housing in Goldsmith Hall on-campus, amidst a larger American cohort. Walking through Front Arch with a few staples* under my arm, seeing the gauntlet of societies laid out before me, I remember just wanting my dad to *go away*. I was ready to throw myself into the deep end of the pool.

And I did. I was out every night, I think. During my time at Trinity, from the beginning, I spent a hell of a lot more time in House 6 than in the library. But that came later. The pool I'd thrown myself into was often adjacent to society life. PolSoc, DU Pubs, Players, some dalliances with LitSoc and the debate societies. And most of all that year, the LGB.† The LGB was in the midst of a somewhat tumultuous year,‡ and I think I became Secretary about a month or two after showing up.§ I was briefly notorious for the simple act of

---

* My first laptop, a CD player from Dixon's and who knows what else.

† Before they added the well-deserved T.

‡ With drama of varieties unnecessary and genuine, much like any other College society.

§ I become President the next year, self-consciously calling myself 'King of the Gays' if asked about it. My name on the LGB website became the source of an unintentional coming out due to a mother with a burgeoning talent for internet stalking.

making society posters in a DIY punk style, slamming text onto homoerotic*
fashion shoots.

At the annual celebration of societies at the end of First Year, I won Fresher
of the Year. I remember the walk to the party, heading towards the south quays
in a pair of red-leather faux-snakeskin pants,†,‡ ignoring abuse shouted at me
on the street. The affair turned out to be a boozy one in a hotel function room,
yet another chance to rub elbows with society heads. The next day, one gloriously clear from a sore head, bits of scandal clattered sticky and warm in my
memory. It felt like the beginning of some bright thing.

But Trinity wasn't all about Bulmers.§ It was also about bad decisions.
Trinity was about feeling alone even when surrounded by dozens of people.
Trinity was about breaking my own heart over and over against the wall of
impossible expectations.¶ Trinity was about making unjustifiably selfish decisions without remorse and failing to guard against inexorable demands on
my personal time or space. It was about unexpected death, men who ignored
boundaries and maudlin hash-fuelled existential crises that I was unable to
explain to my parents.** It was also about an ill-advised foray into politics, in
that I made an unsuccessful run for Entertainment Officer†† and thoroughly
ignored my other obligations.

I imagine it surprised no one who knew me when I was forced to repeat
Second Year.

---

* In that insufferable male gaze-y way that fashion photography used to shoot two femme women making
out.

† Yes, I mean trousers, but it's been fifteen years and my Americanisms are back in full effect. Please enjoy
that brief image of me in red-leather underwear. Yes, brief was a pun.

‡ Pants which I subsequently bequeathed to beloved Dublin icon Tonie Walsh when I headed back to the
States after being summarily denied Irish residency after finishing my degree.

§ I drank *so much* Bulmers, despite everyone around me constantly declaring that they couldn't stand it after
having thrown it up too many times in fields when they were mere youths.

¶ Apologies to everyone I romanced during the serial monogamy years of 2000–5.

** It was also about equally unexplainably abysmal marks in 'Economy of Ireland', even after retaking the exam.

†† I found an old copy of the Piranha election pamphlet recently and was overjoyed to remember that they
referred to me as an 'ill-tempered goblin' or something like that.

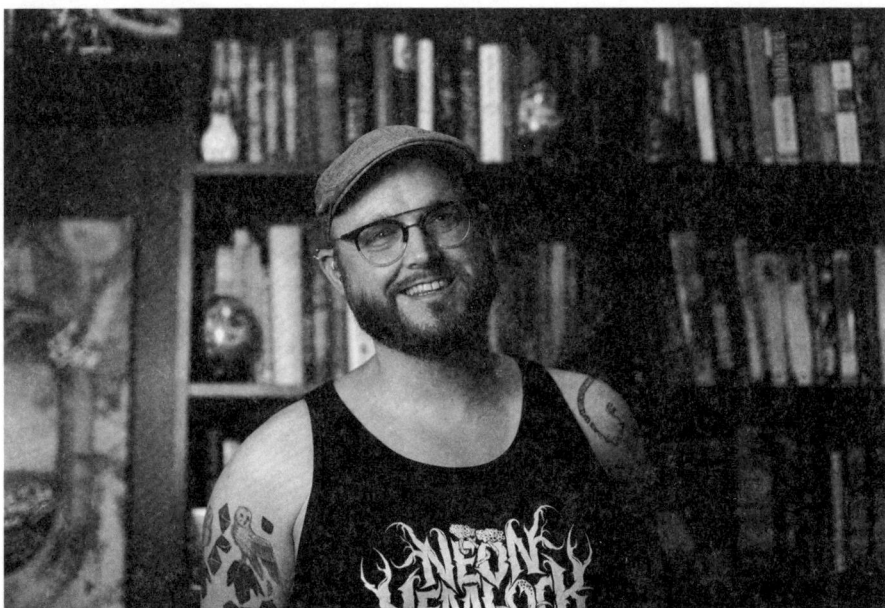

Photo credit: Farrah Skeiky.

I wish* I could say I changed tack after that. Instead, I did the bare minimum to succeed in my courses and slid into other spheres. It galls me a bit now to think about how wholeheartedly and without reservation I inhabited these other identities – DJ, performer, fashion stylist, magazine editor, photographer, model, gee-eyed mess on the dancefloor, nightclub organizer, IDK what else. Half of that in House 6, the other half in various kips throughout Dublin. I would have been hard pressed then to imagine the trajectory I'd end up on. Looking back, it felt like shapeshifting, trying on skins. Trying to figure out what felt most comfortable. There were a few moments where I could have carried on with those threads, but I never followed through. The photoshoot for a big magazine I wasn't brave enough to take on,† the column I took in a petty streak instead of a reflective one.

I'm not sure what prompted my slide into respectability. There was no single moment I can remember, nudging me out of a wobbly orbit into something more stable. But I dug in and did the work. I become a constituent of Club Lecky, photographing armies of dead trees and smoking pack after pack

---

* Do I?

† This was right on the cusp of photography's shift to digital, and I was dragging my heels.

of Camel Lights on the ramp.* I punctuated library time with a gym habit for
the first time in my life, enjoying a brief moment in the sun where I actually
had abs. I somehow pulled off a 2:1 in Fourth Year through a combination of
pure stubbornness, an essay on *Kill Bill*'s subversion of the male gaze† and a
dissertation on men and the embodiment of style.

Still, I managed life at Trinity by making connections. I can't count or
name the friendships I made there that I still hold dear,‡ but they were vital.
I don't think I truly reckoned on the affirmation that I would feel from being
known. It's a simple, heady pleasure, one not easily duplicated the further I get
from those cobblestones.

I visited Dublin in 2006 or so, with my boyfriend at the time. It was
recently enough after college that, on a walk from Ranelagh to O'Connell
Street, we bumped into more than ten folks that I'd known from college or
nightclubs or wherever else. It felt like the proof of the stories I'd told, evidence
that I'd really gotten up to the trouble I'd claimed. Look, here are the folks
yelling across the street, calling my name, saying, 'lo, is it not dave ring? Are
you back from America?'

It's been fourteen years since that visit. At the moment, I'm the publisher
of a small independent press after six years as the director of a sexual assault
hotline. Maybe this skin'll stick for a little while, or maybe I'm still shapeshifting. If I am, hopefully it'll be a hell of a lot more slowly. I've been back to
Dublin more than a handful of times,§ most recently in 2018.¶ We did nearly
that same walk on a beautiful summer evening, though from a friend's place in

---

* Which I hear now is illegal? But I derived so much joy from it. That and Arts Block machine lattes, those
pre-packaged cappuccino muffins and sneaking off to Dunne & Crescenzi with Mairead for the vegetarian
antipasti.

† Which I re-read a couple years ago and completely disagree with now. Incidentally, my professor also
disagreed with me on basically every point, and yet gave me the best marks of my academic career (an 81,
I think?)

‡ And more than that, I love hearing about folks' accomplishments, even the folks I don't stay in touch with.
I had a coronavirus Zoom call recently with some old classmates that I largely don't talk to anymore, and it
was heartwarming and humbling to hear what everyone has gotten up to.

§ One time during a summer visit a couple years ago, I stayed in student housing in Front Square. While
the convenience of location was there, it largely fulfilled whatever the opposite of nostalgia might be called.
I splashed out on a hotel for subsequent visits.

¶ Same guy, we're married now. See, there's a happy ending buried in here.

Dundrum to a hotel just outside College. I still love that city's winding roads, and the light of a late summer day slicing down Dame Street, but I'll admit that my heart fell a little when, the entire way, I didn't see a soul I knew.

dave ring (TCD 2000–5; Sociology and Social Policy) is a queer editor and writer of speculative fiction living in Washington, DC. He is the publisher and managing editor of Neon Hemlock Press, as well as editor of the anthology **Glitter + Ashes: Queer Tales of a World That Wouldn't Die**. His short fiction has been featured in numerous publications, including Fireside Fiction, PodCastle and **A Punk Rock Future**. Find him at dave-ring.com or @slickhop on Twitter.

TEACH ME, I'M IRISH

jonathan schachter

I'M FROM CANADA. My father is Jewish. My mother, born and raised in Galway, left Ireland in the 1960s and converted to Judaism before marrying my dad. It would have been hard for me to imagine someone more strong-willed than she is, but I've become friends with enough Irish women to know that she's probably unexceptional in this regard.

To me, Ireland was just a sort of background fact about my mother. People say she has an accent, but I don't hear it. She has a lot of Irish attributes that I now recognize: she has a way with words, banters with ease, is one of seven, can hold a grudge and likes fruitcake. She has combined Irish guilt and Jewish guilt into a superpower: 'Happy birthday. If you ever feel like calling me, my phone number is on the cheque.'

I went to a Jewish primary school in Toronto, and then to an all-boys, non-denominational high school. In my penultimate year there, I had an English teacher whom I admired immensely. He was brilliant, articulate, polished, more cultured than anyone I had ever met and gay. For a closeted kid at an all-boys school, it was reassuring to know a normal, successful gay man. He spent half the year teaching Irish literature. He observed my nascent curiosity about Ireland and encouraged me to consider going to university in Dublin. He arranged for someone from TCD to visit Toronto to complete the pitch.

My parents hadn't let my sister move to British Columbia for university. Our father, an overprotective dermatologist, worried that she would not wear sunscreen away from home.

Despite this, the idea of going to Dublin intrigued me. It would be an opportunity to explore a part of my identity. Crucially, though, I wanted to move out, be an adult and see the world. I figured that, if I picked Ireland, my mother would love the idea and my dad would have little say. (For whatever reason, he was not worried about my sun safety in Ireland.) It was a solid strategy.

My mother took me to Ireland in the summer before university. I had an Irish passport, but this was my first time setting foot in the country. Her brothers showed me around Galway, told me stories about my grandmother and introduced me to Jameson. My mother and I took a day trip to Dublin. The weather behaved itself, so when we walked through Trinity it captivated me. My mind was made up. I accepted my admission offer and bought a copy of *Dubliners*.

In the autumn, my father and sister came with me to Dublin to help me move. It was nice to have family to help carry my things, but I was itching to be independent, settle into my Pearse Street accommodation and make the most of the fact that in my new life I was of drinking age. At some point, I told them that I would like to try sleeping on-campus rather than at the hotel. It seemed like a big step, and my sister walked me to Front Gate where, because I had not signed her in, security refused to admit us.

The rooms on Pearse Street were small and resembled a cabin on a ship. The shared kitchen was tiny. My dad and sister helped me furnish the place and buy the necessities that I couldn't pack. We bought a mini-fridge because we were genuinely unable to find a fridge in the kitchen. As it turned out, in an industrial design misstep, it was attached to the stove, and would warm up whenever the stove was on.

At first, I was more excited than nervous. Everything seemed slightly foreign and amusing. I made a Freshers' Week friend from Derry, whom I told more than once, 'I have no idea what you are saying to me right now.'

Within a month, I began to question my move. While 2002 does not feel like all that long ago, the world has shrunk considerably since then. There was no Facebook or Skype or Gmail. Keeping in touch with home was more difficult and costly than it is now. Homesickness set in as the days grew shorter and the cold rain unremittingly battered the window of my tiny room. Dublin can feel grim in December. Reading *Dubliners* did not help.

Everyone spoke of 'soft rain'. In Toronto, rain is occasional but torrential, and it usually ends soon after it begins. Dublin rain was different. Some days, it was like walking through mist. When it was windy, the rain fell sideways. This was new to me. When the rain lifted, the rubbish bins overflowed with broken umbrellas. I loved this. If the Irish won't invent a better umbrella, who will?

I enrolled in History and Political Science. We were lumped with Philosophy and Political Science. We – about twenty of us – were told that the programmes were prestigious, and their students had the reputation of being competitive. My classmates were impressive. Everyone was friendly, but they were intimidatingly knowledgeable, opinionated and intelligent, and it filled me with self-doubt.

I put up with relentless but good-hearted jabs at Canada. I eventually ordered a book called *Canada Firsts* and its sequel, *More Canada Firsts*, to answer the most common question: what has Canada ever done? In exchange, everyone put up with my questions about Ireland. Questions such as: what's a 'carvery'? And why do people say 'now' when they give you a beer? Why mark courses out of 100, if the maximum score is 79? What's the deal with the Angelus? And how do I get on *Winning Streak*?

To the Irish, there must be nothing less interesting than a guy with an American accent exploring his Irish roots. I think they see it as more genuine, however, if you're willing to pay rent in Dublin. And they are a bit more forgiving with Canadians.

I moved to Ireland to be more Irish, but in my group I became the most Jewish. My friends had no shortage of questions about Jews. This was my first time meeting people who had never met a Jew before. I answered as many questions as I could – far more circumcision-related questions than I could have expected. For the most part, however, my Jewish identity took a backseat. I was Canadian, living in Ireland and learning about Irishness through immersion. I felt settled, but never local.

I should have spent more time exploring Irish food than Irish drink. Instead, it was a year of yoghurt and Pot Noodle – things I could eat straight from my mini-fridge, or prepare with my bedroom kettle, to avoid the kitchen – and the student special at the Buttery. Even in a college cafeteria, things felt slightly foreign. I remember laughing when I asked what the special was and was told, 'It's fowl.' 'I have no doubt,' I replied, 'but I'd still like to know what it is.'

HistPol and PhilPol took the library tour together. The Ussher was brand new, and the librarian bragged that it had passed a suicide study. A Kilkenny girl from PhilPol asked me, 'Is it just me, or do you feel like the third tit in a small bra?' She put up with my questions ('What's slippage?', etc.). Her gregarious laugh – and ability to find humour in anything – put me at ease. Sure, the Ussher was nice, but no one on earth likes Brutalism and an orange/brown colour story more than I do, so I was more impressed with the Arts Block and its tiny, windowless seminar rooms.

It wasn't long before I had terrific friends, mainly in History, History and Political Science, Philosophy and Political Science, and Law. Contrary to widespread rumours of hyper-competition between students in my program, my classmates were supportive, collaborative and generally hilarious, and their interest in our courses (even the most boring of them) was energizing.

Our lecturers were like nothing I had ever experienced. I took a course on early-modern Europe delivered by a captivating historian who would dress as a witch for her lecture on witch-hunts. I had a sort of academic crush on her. My classmates did not believe me, but I was certain that she made regular eye contact with me in class. Once, when we bumped into each other in the Arts Block, she told me that she recognized me from her lectures: 'Always in the back row, beside the exit, with that big mop of red hair.'* Lecturers, she told me, often pick a person to lecture to. This vindicated what I'd been telling people, but also highlighted a recurring theme in my travels: I really don't blend in abroad.

Other Irish idiosyncrasies fascinated and amused me. On the political science side, our First Year lectures were shared with BESS. Because of the number of students, we were divided into seminars alphabetically by surname. Because of a timetable conflict, I was lumped in with one of *two* groups

---

* The red hair was a decision that I now know was a mistake.

for surnames starting with O. The roll-call always made me smile: O'Brien, O'Connor, O'Connor, O'Connor, O'Donohue. Only in Ireland.

In my second year, I moved to a flat in Ringsend with a classmate from the United States. For a brief period, our neighbours regarded us – two blow-ins – with suspicion. Over time, they became protective of us. It seemed again like the Irish were more patient with visitors who demonstrated an intent to stay a while. We got to know the people at the local shops and chipper, as my diet evolved from powdered soups, without becoming any healthier. It was a year of oven pizzas, curry chips and frozen Capri Sun.

Many of my classmates decided to sit the scholarship examinations. I was told that, if I sat it too, I could finish the year early, and maybe explore a bit of Europe. We understood that one HistPol student, maximum, could be elected, which managed our expectations. Preparation was stressful, particularly with the niggling possibility that I would have to sit end-of-year exams if I under-performed. But it was exciting to be among motivated students who were exploring their academic interests.

The exams, and particularly the History general paper, were formative. The general paper was untethered to any course and, we were told, tested for 'flair'. It had a list of questions like 'Tribunals', 'Unity in Diversity' and 'What if?' The History department had given us license to read whatever we wanted. I studied high school history notes in an effort to pass as an Irish student with an unusual awareness of the Mexican Revolution; and I read off-beat articles about things like the demographics of opioid use in early twentieth-century America. I came to the general paper not knowing what to expect,* and left the exam feeling quite uncertain but invigorated. I think my classmates felt the same way. Three of us (of six or so) were elected from HistPol.

Trinity Monday ought to have been a day free from self-doubt, an impor-tant milestone in the exploration of my academic identity. Instead, however, another new scholar introduced herself to me as a *Foundation* scholar in some hard science ('the hardest scholarship to get', and in 'the hardest subject', she

---

* This was the year that Ireland proudly became the first country to ban tobacco indoors, so I should have predicted that 'The Tobacco Ban' would be a question. I remember relying on the opioid article to make the case that tobacco control becomes possible when tobacco becomes less prevalent among elites.

explained). 'Therefore …' she concluded about her own relative intellect. I rolled my eyes, but the doubt returned.

Ultimately, Schols' biggest impact was on accommodation. It makes student life more settled because you are not moving around the city from year to year; however, you live in a bubble, largely with international students, athletes and (other) nerds. There is so much about Dublin life that you may miss from within that bubble.

In my third year, the Accommodation Office put me in the GMB on a floor with six women, including a bunch of scholars a year ahead of me, and the vice president of the Students' Union. It was strange to be the only guy. I suppose a straight college student might think the opportunity was wasted on me, but it did introduce me to people from other disciplines. I'm not very intimidating to women, and I'm certain my diet alarmed them, so they took care of me.

I took a specialized course on the Weimar Republic. It is probably the most fascinating course I have ever taken. The lecturer encouraged us to explore our interests, and I focused on themes of economic anxiety, the 'modern woman' of interwar Germany and subversive art. Several years ago, at a wedding in Toronto, I bumped into an Irish classmate from that seminar who said he remembered my presentation about depictions of war injuries and sexual murder in Weimar art. I'm glad to have made an impression.

Around Third Year, more friends began to visit from home, and I began to explore the country with greater vigour. I would take visitors to the Giant's Causeway, Slieve League or the Ring of Kerry, and always on the Dublin Literary Pub Crawl. I forced Irish butter, milk and cheese on any visitor who would eat it.* Even if Ireland was not my country, it had indelibly become part of my story, and I was proud to show it off.

As the end of the degree approached, I began to feel that I had squandered my European adventure. I amped up my travels to see as much of the continent as I could.

In my final year of the BA, I moved into Botany Bay with a close friend from PhilPol. He remains one of the most knowledgeable people I have ever met. Nonetheless, PhilPol failed to engage him, and he left TCD without

---

* If anyone from the Dairy Board is reading: when I graduated from frozen pizzas, I became your most loyal ambassador, and I would like to discuss opportunities for expansion into the Canadian market.

completing the programme. Our apartment was large and bright. With our own kitchen and more fridge space per capita, and probably resulting from a year with maternal flatmates who got me past junk food, I cooked and ate like a normal human. As I explained in a complaint letter to Dunnes (in respect of a price hike on Toscanella mozzarella balls from €0.69 to €0.90!), ours was a salad-oriented household.

Our flat became a hub for PhilPol and HistPol buddies to pop over and waste days watching *Countdown*, *Wife Swap*, *Paisean Faisean*, MTV's *My Super Sweet 16* or whatever programming Channel 4 had to offer about people with unusual medical conditions. We stayed up senselessly late and talked utter shite. We joked, for example, about suggesting wine pairings on the title pages of our assignments.

One friend, Pete, made our place his second home. As early-morning delirium set in, we would joke about the stupidest things. We brainstormed names for funny musicals, all but one of which would never be produced. Pete and I thought 'Chairs (Musical)', a musical about musical chairs, would be funny. Pete wrote most of it, gave me a co-writer credit, and the IFB provided funding for him to produce it and debut it at the Galway Film Fleadh. I accepted Pete's dare to include the term 'lemon-shaped rock', a *Simpsons* reference, in an essay.[*] My greatest accomplishment at Trinity was, surely, that our professor gave me a first on that essay and used the word 'lemonality' throughout his comments. Facebook was in its crude infancy, and people's walls were static pages that listed favourite movies and books. Pete and I thought it criminal that Trinity's favourite book was not the Book of Kells, so we set up a group called 'Book of Kells … my favourite book', with crudely drawn pictures and fake book reviews. It never took off, but it was funny to us.

The History general paper imbued in me an interest in tobacco-control policy. I wrote my undergraduate dissertation on the subject, and with the encouragement of my supervisor applied to the PhD program in political science to conduct research in this area.

---

[*] On the topic 'democracy is an essentially contested concept', I argued that democracy was like 'lemonality', and different instantiations of democracy, whether American or Swiss or ancient Greek may in some way be lemony. Much like lemons, pink lemonade and a lemon-shaped rock can each claim to have some lemony element.

I continued my postgraduate education at TCD for three years. I had more low lows and fewer high highs as a postgraduate than as an undergraduate. I was anxious about the uncertain end date of the PhD. As the editors of this book will tell you, I do not work well without a deadline. Instead, I opted to submit my dissertation as a Masters when Schols and IRCHSS funding came to an end.

I made an enemy of an imperious Law-student flatmate in the GMB who arrived two months late and insisted on disturbing how we (who arrived on time) distributed the kitchen storage. Before long, Shelf Girl would become one of my closest Irish friends. Our friendship was dysfunctional and lovely, and I was lucky to live with her for my remaining years in Dublin. We spent far too many nights on the town with her friends, often followed by hours at Front Gate bantering with Mic and the gang at security.

Initially, the workload was overwhelming. My department was gradually recasting my research topic beyond recognition. I felt that one of my lecturers singled me out, and was asking others in the department about my sexuality. Luckily, I had friends in the department – a fabulous Polish researcher ahead of me, and a born Irish politician in my class – as sources of support, but I eventually transferred to a different department.

Funding allowed Shelf Girl and me to afford frills, like travel and good food. For me, IRCHSS might as well have been a scheme to redistribute money from the Irish government to a restaurant called Maloti, predominantly for the purchase of a dish called Khazana Murgh. Sorry.

In early January of my final year, Shelf Girl and I celebrated her friend's birthday at Legg's, a second home for her group. On our return, a group of teenagers stopped us to ask us for a lighter. Shelf Girl jokingly asked if they were on their way home from their First Communion. One of them asked if I was a faggot. I said yes. One of them sucker punched me and kicked me to the ground. They beat the shit out of me before running off. Covered in my own blood, I called 999. Twice. Each time, the operator told me that it was not an appropriate emergency. I was encouraged to walk to my local Garda station. Defeated, I walked to the station on Pearse Street, gave a statement, and took a cab, still covered in blood, to the nearest A&E. It was light out by the time a nurse sewed up the 'through-and-through gash' on my face.

I knew my time in Dublin was coming to an end. The attack, and more particularly what felt like a betrayal by 999, made the transition a bit easier. I complained to the Ombudsman, which ultimately found in my favour that the 999 operators were 'unprofessional', 'failed to follow Standard Operating Procedures' and had 'a disciplinary case to answer', resulting in a significantly lower 'chance of apprehending those responsible for the attack'. The Chief Superintendent considered this report and declined to take further action. I was advised that there was nothing further that I could do.

My Irish adventure was rapidly coming to an end. In my last week, with my crap shipped off,* I was able to relax a bit and process what was happening. My friends arranged for a going-away party at Maloti. Shelf Girl managed to get me the recipe for Khazana Murgh. 'Wouldn't it be funny,' I asked, 'if it was ketchup and spices?' And, of course, it had ketchup in it.

On my last morning in Dublin, I was ready to move on to my new adventure at the University of Toronto. It was sad, but it was time. My friends deposited me at the airport, and I updated my status on Facebook: 'I will arise and go now, and go to U of T.'

Jonathan Schachter (TCD 2002–6, History and Political Science; 2006–9, MLitt) is from Toronto, Canada. He visited Ireland for the first time in 2002 and stayed for seven years. He was a Foundation Scholar and gold medallist in history and political science before returning home to pursue a degree in Law. He is an avid complainer and practises as a plaintiff-side class action litigator, primarily in consumer protection, in Toronto.

---

* In my experience, Irish people love to give box-loads of Catholic tat to Jews.

CHANGING TRINITY, CHANGING THE WORLD

A PERSONAL REFLECTION

rory hearne

I HAD NEVER BEEN inside the gates of Trinity College before I walked in as a seventeen-year-old First Year science student in 1996. I was the quintessential culchie, having grown up working on my father's small farm in the town of Tramore, Co. Waterford. In my first few weeks I connected with other culchies in my science classes. One guy, Brecan, who was from Clare, became a good friend. We shared an interest in hurling and social justice, and a dislike of Fianna Fáil. There was also a fiery girl from Armagh, a big, kind Mayo farmer and a socialist from Meath. But in the first few days in Dublin, I got a quick introduction to the harsh inequalities of the city when I was mugged by a guy with a blade on Ha'penny Bridge. Back inside the walls of Trinity, I met privileged cliques and private-school-educated students as well as others like me from ordinary backgrounds, who, because of the introduction of free education in 1996, had university opened up to us. I had gone to school in a local Christian Brothers School and had friends from a cross-section of social backgrounds, but I had never witnessed the gap in social class that I saw in Trinity and its surrounding areas. In Freshers' Week, I joined the St Vincent de Paul Society and began tutoring disadvantaged primary school children in Westland Row CBS on Pearse Street. Here I saw the challenges of inner-city deprivation.

As part of my Natural Science degree, I took courses on microbiology and genetics. I questioned the lecturer about genetic modification of crops and about corporations benefitting to the detriment of farmers and nature. I took courses in geography on the development of class societies, with lecturer Mark Hennessy opening my mind up to a new understanding of empires and colonies, third-world poverty and capitalism. As the son of a small farmer involved with co-ops, I connected with the inequality of land ownership in Latin America. I was angered by US intervention in overthrowing democratically elected governments in the interests of US corporations. I studied environmental protection and had inspiring lectures on public house-building programmes of affordable, mixed-income and well-planned homes by the uber-intelligent Marxist, Andrew MacLaran.

Over the summer of my second year, while working on our farm, I read the political philosophy notes from a friend who studied BESS. I gobbled up Rousseau and Plato's *Republic*. I bought a sociology textbook by Anthony Giddens from the Trinity SU bookshop and was fascinated by its analysis of inequality, Marxism and Weber. In my third and fourth years, I was fortunate, given the flexibility of Trinity's programme, to do modules in Economics and Sociology, and I dropped the Natural Science modules. Professor P.J. Drudy from the Economics department imparted his incredible depth of knowledge on housing economics and inequality, which informs and inspires my current work. My lecturers were educators who gave us great time and support. They were not under the pressure many of us academics experience today in the neoliberal university, where the focus has shifted to research funding and publishing with teaching losing out, at times to the detriment of the students' educational experience.

I took part in my first protest in Second Year. My strong opposition to corruption (my dad had spent a lot of time shouting at Charlie Haughey on the TV), and the golden circle of banks, politicians and developers meant that when Brecan invited me to a march against the road planned for the Glen of the Downs, I happily joined in with my hand-drawn banner that read 'Fianna Fáil – the Builders Party'.

I went to debates at the Hist and the Phil on politics and human rights, but mostly watched on, as I had never even taken part in a school's debate before – we just didn't have them. But I was annoyed by how these polished, well-spoken students would debate any issue, on any side. It was all just a game to them. For me, if you were taking a side or a perspective, you did it because you believed in it. Motivated to highlight injustices, I took the podium and debated the trained debaters.

I got involved in the One World Society to highlight third-world poverty and indebtedness, to decry multinationals' sweatshop clothes factories and to support East Timor. I became friends with a lovely student from Germany who invited me to visit his home. So, in the summer of 1999, and using my savings from working in a tile-assembly factory on Pearse Street, I took my first trip outside of Ireland to visit Cologne. While there, we went to the anti-G8 Summit protest, and I was inspired as thousands of people marched for global and environmental justice.

STUDENTS' UNION

My studies were going very well, and a few friends suggested I run for President of the Students' Union. My girlfriend at the time, who I had met in Second Year when we were leafleting for opposing Students' Union presidential candidates, also encouraged me. I remember thinking I wanted to raise the issues of educational inequality. We ran the campaign like a social movement, with a large group of student activists from diverse left political backgrounds: environmentalists, socialists and my friends from the hurling and athletics clubs. We were mainly outsiders, and we all wanted change. My manifesto called for college to be more student-oriented and for 'Education as a right – not a privilege'. I highlighted the cost of living, accommodation crisis, inadequate grants, registration fees and the lack of access to third-level for those from disadvantaged backgrounds. My manifesto included a photo of me protesting against Bertie Ahern when he had visited the university in 1999, with the caption 'Rory tells Bertie it's time for change.'

We wanted to make student politics more activist-oriented rather than just a social club for insiders. I hoped to get students to be more active politically as well, to make a better college and better wider society.

I was elected, and we had one hell of a party that night.

In July 2000, I had just started my role as SU President when I got a phone call from my mother telling me Dad wasn't well. I visited him in Waterford Regional Hospital. He had been diagnosed with a brain tumour. He seemed upbeat, and though it was upsetting, as far as I was told, the treatment would work. I hadn't the faintest clue of the gravity of the situation.

Back in Trinity, the first few weeks of August were incredibly exciting. I even got my first mobile phone with the job. The sabbatical officer team (myself, Joe Davitt as Deputy President and Editor of the *University Record*, Karen Griffin as Welfare Officer, Averil Power as Education Officer and Timmy Carty the Ents Officer) bonded well, planned out our year and really gelled. We got fantastic support from Simon Evans, the manager of the SU. I remember folding leaflets for Freshers' Week, the sun shining down on a quiet Front Square, while we pumped out Bob Dylan, 'It Ain't Me Babe' and 'The Times They Are a-Changing'. I was loving the role and looking forward to the year ahead, campaigning for education and social justice, and enjoying life. I had no inkling of what would unfold over the next few months, personally and as an activist, and how it would change me as a person, leaving a darkness that would take many years to lift and get over.

In early September 2000, myself and Joe Davitt attended the huge anti-globalization protests at the IMF and the World Bank Global Summits in Prague. We went as an SU delegation calling for cancellation of third-world debt and for workers' and students' rights. We were part of peaceful protests but were confronted by riot police who baton-charged the crowd. As we attempted to escape, I was arrested and treated roughly in the Czech prison where I was held, without sleep for thirty hours, and strip-searched. I was terrified there.

My concern for my father's situation, along with my focus on the role of President, meant that I didn't take in, or process, what had happened to me at the protests and the Czech prison. I didn't consider how disconnected my experience was from regular students in Trinity.

MY FATHER'S PASSING

Unfortunately, during this time, my father's cancer worsened. I visited him in hospital in Waterford in late September 2000, and he told me with a wry smile that he had seen the anti-IMF protests on TV and knew that I was there – even though I hadn't told him I was going. Typical of Dad's generation, open declarations of love or pride were rare, but a friend of his told me subsequently of my beaming dad, bounding up to him and telling him proudly that his son had become President of TCDSU. During October, I travelled to Cork University Hospital where he went for chemotherapy treatment. I could not comprehend that he was losing his battle with cancer and that he actually might die. I just assumed he was going to recover. But he died on 3 November 2000.

I was utterly devastated, ripped up from the inside out. I was so angry that he was taken away from me. It changed me. I turned off inside, unable to deal with the loss. I ran away from the grief and turned away from those who cared for me. I didn't get any grief counselling, though looking back I badly needed it. It wasn't until a few years later, when I was back in Trinity doing my PhD in 2007, that I availed of college counselling and began a long process of unlocking and healing the grief and other hurt.*

BACK TO STUDENT ACTIVISM

After the Prague protests, I moved quickly to focus the Union activity on key student issues, such as campaigning for the Trinity Access Programme, which provides a pathway for those from marginalized and disadvantaged backgrounds to access Trinity. We highlighted the student accommodation crisis, and I maintain that if our calls for direct state investment in campus accommodation, rent controls and tenants' rights had been enacted, the housing crisis would not be as bad today. We set up an intercultural programme involving foreign students in activities with inner-city primary schools to promote intercultural relations and challenge racism. I took part in protests in support of asylum seekers.

It was daunting being a twenty-year-old running the entire Students' Union, which included a travel agent, three shops and over twenty staff. I worked to ensure the staff were included more in the Union, had better wages and were supported if they looked to go back to education. The monthly SU Council

---

* That the Trinity counselling was available free of charge was important to enable me to take it up, as I was on a research grant and couldn't afford private therapy. It highlights the importance of freely available mental-health support services for students and the wider public.

meetings (where I had to present my work reports and plans) usually had 100 or so elected student representatives from across the university. They were nerve-wracking and exciting. There was ferocious debate over the direction of the Union – which is what I had hoped to achieve in increasing participation of students. I also set up a SU student activist campaigning group that was open for all students – not just class reps. Some class reps were more interested in organizing class parties. While these were important social events, I believed the Students' Union should be a place to progress ideals and values, solidarity and change. For me, it was always about trying to rattle the cage, shake up the institutions and break down walls and barriers to include those excluded.

We succeeded in shifting the Students' Union to more direct action. In November, we organized a boycott of the Buttery in protest at a 6 per cent increase in catering prices. It was the first time a boycott had been organized in Trinity for two decades (the last one was done while Joe Duffy was SU President). We met the Provost, and he agreed to defer the price increases and give students greater input into decision-making.

The editorial of the *Trinity News* criticized the shift to direct action but said, 'The threatened boycott of the Buttery has been a timely reminder that a combination of wit and calculated disorder can lead to success and success it was ... the College now know that they must be more considered in their approach to students.'

In December, I proposed a motion to the SU Council to participate in the occupation of a government department as part of the national students' grants campaign. It was seconded by the really hard-working and always compassionate Welfare Officer, Karen Griffin, but opposed by the deter-mined Education Officer, Averil Power. The motion passed, and I took part in the occupation of the Department of Enterprise and Trade. We barricaded ourselves in using the furniture and hung a banner out the window. After a few hours, the Guards literally smashed the door down with an axe to get in. It had echoes of 'Here's Johnny!' from *The Shining*.

Trinity Students' Union had not been a member of USI, the national student's union, since 1992, and there was vocal opposition to re-joining. The SU Council voted against a motion I tabled to hold a referendum to re-affiliate to USI. The SU campaign committee and I then collected 350 signatures which meant a referendum could be held. A majority of students voted to re-join in the referendum, and we proudly returned Trinity to be part of the national student's union movement.

PhD 2004–9

I started a PhD in the Department of Geography in Trinity in 2004, researching inequality associated with neoliberalism and privatization of public services. My case studies included social housing communities in Dublin being regenerated through Public–Private Partnerships. I continued my student activism in Trinity, supported by the Central Societies Committee. I spearheaded the successful Trinity Boycott Coke Campaign in support of the Colombian Coca-Cola workers, whose trade union was highlighting their suffering of alleged human rights abuses by Coca-Cola. Trinity students voted in favour of banning Coca-Cola products from Students' Union shops – with 1,800 supporting the ban and 1,600 against. I then successfully stood for Campaigns Officer and Deputy President of USI that same year. I took a year out from the PhD for that role, and we vigorously campaigned against the return of student fees and further cutbacks. I asked at the time, 'What education system will be left in ten years after these cutbacks?' We see the answer today in the underfunding crisis in higher education. Just like in housing, austerity cuts and the failure to invest leave a detrimental legacy for decades. We opposed government plans to introduce antisocial behaviour orders and called to invest in facilities for young people instead, and I organized anti-war protests.

My first son, Leo, was born in October of 2004, bringing me great joy and a new perspective on life. Being a father changed me again, seeing the world through the eyes of a parent, thinking longer term of the life and world we make for our children.

TRINITY IS A UNIQUE PLACE FULL OF OUR MEMORIES

I completed my PhD in 2009, with massive support from my wonderful wife (who, I have to admit, is a graduate of UCD). I continue campaigning on homelessness and for a right to housing for all. I've also been a researcher, policy analyst, media commentator (I even do a politics podcast – 'Reboot Republic'), and I've written a book on PPPs and this year published one on the housing crisis, *Housing Shock*. Trinity played a strong role in nurturing my passion and commitment to social justice, and empowering me with knowledge to follow this path. I feel a strong affinity and sense of gratitude for that.

A geographical imaginary emphasizes the importance of unique places, and how the people and spaces create those places. Trinity is one such place that has a strong sense of place and community. Through the arch of Trinity, you enter another city, with its own walls and its particular history of exclusion and inclusion.

I return to Trinity and walk through the gates every few months and use the new alumni coffee room. The ghosts of old friends and relationships still hang around the old grey buildings. I hear the voices of those times echoing across the cobblestones in Front Square. I bump into them sometimes. They are there. In their place. I feel twinges of sadness and regret – but also pride in what we achieved – when I stop and look around in Trinity. The time passes and our time ends, but inside these walls and rooms new dreams are being created. I like to think our echoes remain in the ether, in the stories, in this book – and hopefully might inspire the future generations of student activists and leaders. I hope they will be educated and empowered as I was, their idealism and desire for positive radical change nurtured rather than quenched with cynicism and apathy.

I've been writing this in the middle of the COVID-19 pandemic, with my little sixteen-month-old smiling up at me (and doing a bit of yelling too), and my five- and six-year-old running around as dinosaurs. The future seems more uncertain and frightening for all of us. But they need us to keep working to make sure it is the best future possible for everyone. There's always hope.

In memory of my dear friend from Co. Clare, Brecan Mooney, who died tragically in November 2009.

Dr Rory Hearne (TCD 1996–2000, Natural Sciences; 2004–9 PhD) is an Assistant Professor in Social Policy in the Department of Applied Social Studies Maynooth University. He is author of **Housing Shock: The Irish Housing Crisis and How to Solve It** (2020, Policy Press). He is host of the 'Reboot Republic' podcast and is involved in advocacy relating to homelessness, the right to housing and social justice.

LOW BUNS

kate kennedy

THROUGH TOTAL NAÏVETÉ and sheer jaeger-bombedness, my first few months in Dublin were a scattergun haze of losing things. I presumed that every social venue I went to had a handy stool, corner or floor that I could doggedly lay my belongings on before collecting them eight hours later – sweatier, blurrier and dripping in garlic cheesy chips. And, unfortunately for me – and my peers' street safety – I was right.

It was a total stroke of luck that my pay-as-you-go Meteor SIM turned up days after I dropped it down one of the Pav's crevices. Or that the one winter coat Mum had made me promise to keep safe made its way back to me because 'no other woman in Dublin has arms the length of oars'. By being Dublin's biggest birdbrain, I had accidentally set a tone for Trinity that I've never shaken. No, not alcoholism – although I can see how I've opened this – but an unwavering support system. A bespoke positivity – not a Ned Flanders-esque broken record of buoyancy – but a sturdy foundation of optimistic community. Trinity taught me that the world was spiralling out of control, but that its spirals are 'frightfully stunning, aren't they?' And that there'll always be someone, who knows someone, who knows someone else, who can offer some sort of solace. Thankfully, my scattergun approach to nights out soon waned as I learned to eat pesto pasta before I left Halls and close my zips.

I arrived at Trinity a hop, skip and a wallop after the financial crash. My classmates' parents, who had propped up Trinity twenty years ago, were drenched in employment the millisecond they graduated. We, the pie-eyed millennials, signed up knowing we were screwed. And if you were an arts student, you were artfully job-dodger screwed.

In the first year, however, this rarely crossed our minds. We were faithful to the hope that things would clean themselves up upon our exit. As the job fairs came and went, and the graduate schemers dangled perks in front of the lucky few maths students in the Hamilton building, we sniggered – that was *such* a Fourth Year problem. After all, we'd be graduating in 2012. I'd go back to London and get a job smoothing over the sandpit in the Olympics or something. Easy.

Anyway, I was too busy perfecting my 'neigh' as Boxer the Horse in *Animal Farm*. Trinity's Players Society, the quagmire of thesps, was the backbone of my time at Trinity. Sometimes acting in three plays in one week, I'd spend more time in that wooden treehouse than my own bed. My hair permanently in a low bun, ready to play man, animal or plant. Admittedly I *was* studying a degree in Theatre and Drama, and I am perpetually grateful to the mentorship from Nick Johnson, Brian Singleton, Eric Weiss and Steve Wilmer – the four very different seasons of Man and Professor.

Four years were spent trying to balance learning from our wonderful professors whilst ogling the charcoal portrait of Samuel Beckett in the tutorial room. Christ on a bike, what a creviced, handsome man. I hadn't realized this when I applied to Trinity during my A Levels, innocently thinking his words were his USP. Many a morning tutorial was spent locking eyes with his strikingly intelligent gaze while trying to cover up the fact that my own intelligence had been wrestled and muted by a serious hangover.

The culprit of many a hangover was Players – which was more of a lifestyle than a society. You didn't have to get involved, you just had to be around. And from astronomical odds, ten years later, a lot of us are still around. It's bizarre to think we are all still in the field in some way. It stomps on the odds of a classical drama school training. But the Trinity lot I had the pleasure of encountering seem united in their sparkliness. They have that annoying, indescribable sparkle that the Irish seem to be fed through the placenta. And then they enter the world running. They don't even really run – they amble magnetically and the rest of the world are swept into their vortex.

A prime example of this special talent tincture is Aaron Heffernan. He happened to fall upon a small but spookily accurate impression of Barack Obama in our second year. It was then decided Aaron should run for student president as Obama, accompanied by an in-depth campaign and all its trimmings. Steeped in fake security, with actor Jack Gleeson and rugby captain Scott LaValla in sunglasses and wielding VIP clipboards, the finished product resulted in Aaron/Obama shaking hands with Queen Elizabeth II on her visit to Dublin. *The Late Late Show* quickly scooped him up for Friday night entertainment. The dominoes kept falling; the lads turned this experience into a musical called *Obamamia*, which they played to sold-out audiences at the Edinburgh Fringe. Nearly two years' worth of entertainment from one gag.

Speaking of snowballing, Players were also responsible for the Gumball Challenge, a fundraising event for one of the society musicals where they set a series of challenges, which included 'get a tattoo' or 'get naked in a phonebooth'. 2009 got out of hand when the 'see how far you can travel for free' challenge was taken literally, and a student ended up on a plane to Brisbane.

Halls, the residence for First Years in Rathmines, was the other breeding ground for recalls. It was a hot pot of chaos. Unfortunately for our year, a group of English boys in the year above had been caught up – sorry, homemade the net, thrown it out to sea and dragged it back in – in a scandal that had them forcibly removed from the residence. Their debauchery meant we were under lock and key. I was fined for emptying bottles in the recycling bin too loudly at around 7.30 pm.

Nights out were the be all and end all in those first two years. I missed the third year on an exchange at Berkeley, California where the drinking capacity of my classmates plummeted. I was suddenly on weekend hikes and meeting for green juices before class in the mornings. But, prior to my absence, I had thrown myself knees-deep into the pinnacle event of every year: the Trinity Ball. Tickets were expensive. Girls wore dresses that wouldn't be out of place at the BAFTAs. Certain parents held posh pre-drinks in their polished gardens in Blackrock. It had all the elements of a being a refined and classy affair. Quite the contrary – it was the safari of Trinity. I ran a factory of fake tan, a phenomenon that the Irish gifted to us English girls. My mitts were sodden with the dark stuff, rubbing brown goo on two, perhaps three backs at a time to ensure everyone looked like they had just jumped out of an overzealous toastie machine.

The shaded animals ran wild, six-inch heels broken in the mud whilst smuggling Capri Suns filled with vodka in our bras, bones bruised in the mosh pit to Dizzee Rascal and dozens and dozens of blurry disposable-camera pictures taken outside the Portaloos. Jessie J – the headliner in 2011 – mentioned it was her 'hardest gig to date'. I can only presume she meant the Ash Cloud ... The evening itself was always anticlimactic; it was the months of expectation we loved. The planning got us through revision and coursework as the sun started to reveal its face during the summer term. The challenge was getting through the real thing. A multilingual, goddess-looking friend of mine – now mother and mogul – managed to make the ball for all of fifty-nine seconds before she was escorted out.

The periphery characters of Trinity are incarcerated in my memory. The butcher's daughter who I lived with in Halls, the flies taking over our kitchen after she left too many trays of her dad's rashers in the fridge. The girl that cried out of the window in Front Square to a lad that had wet her bed and then asked for her number, 'It's 085-F*CK OFF.' Ann Murray, who always let me borrow a stapler when I was late for a deadline. The Texan who would frequent the basement bar at Coppers and never take his coat off, who I presumed was the tallest man in Ireland at the time and subsequently the only option for a smooch.

One November evening, I remember hunkering down in Murphy's to watch one of my brothers, second row for London Irish Nick Kennedy, make his debut, his 'cap' for England against the Pacific Islanders. The pub was littered with friends I had managed to scoop up those first few months after we'd recovered from the Freshers' flu. My heart leapt out of my mouth when, in slow motion, I saw Nick in his red scrum cap cross over the line with the ball in his arms. It was a kind of pride I'd never felt before, and I turned to the motley crew behind me. Every one of them were on their feet, on the table, celebrating as if it was their big brother. It didn't matter that it was the wrong international team. Ten years on, I still receive messages from that lot whenever they see him on TV.

Trinity scored my twenties, and as I turn thirty I don't see it going off-piste. My first love was an ex-Trinity student, and I played the priest at two

Trinity weddings last year. For the last half-decade, my flat in London has been a conveyor belt of Trinity. One is out, another one arrives, binning my PG Tips and packing the shelves with Barry's. And, without a doubt, Trinity is the reason I'm still working in theatre. So the award (and the blame) for a lifetime of low buns and lying to my family that the show will be 'definitely be less than an hour' goes to … Trinity.

Photo credit: Wil Coban.

Kate Kennedy (TCD 2008–12; Drama and Theatre Studies) is an actress and writer based in London, currently in Budapest filming the **Halo** TV series for Spielberg's company Amblin Television. After studying at Trinity, Kate trained at RADA (Royal Academy of Dramatic Art) in the UK. In theatre, she has performed in **Epiphany and Furniture** (Druid Theatre); **Twelfth Night** (Royal Exchange); **The Cat's Mother** and **Hunch** (Edinburgh Fringe); NYT REP West End Season (West End). Her TV appearances include **Handy** (RTÉ); **A Midsummer Night's Dream** (BBC); **Catastrophe** (Channel 4).

THE STANFORD MARSHMALLOW EXPERIMENT

darragh mccausland

NOT FOR ONE moment during that first academic year did I feel I belonged there. My memories from First Year of single honours Psychology are full of me sitting among people who looked at me like I was a variety of mundane pest that eats lovely English flowers. The caterpillar of a common butterfly maybe. This general feeling began in the jumbled chaos of my start of term and never quite lifted. At least not until the summer, when I took a job working with a conglomeration of misfits in the housekeeping department. But that is to race ahead to another tale entirely. It would be nice to race ahead. You see, even now, when I recall my beginnings in Trinity, wheeling around and around on the sodden carousel of Freshers' Week, I am confronted with a contradictory stillness, a frieze of frozen memories of such shame that to experience them brings on pangs of physical discomfort. Each panel luridly lit. Each filled with enough horror to put me off my breakfast twenty years later.

On the first night of Freshers' Week, I blundered up Marlborough Street towards the college after 'pre-drinks' in the wet-cardboard-scented Parnell Street flat I shared with a fellow bog boy who had taken to his place of study, DIT, like a duck to water. I was a different story. Earlier that day, I felt surprisingly lonely as I bounced aimlessly among the society stalls, excruciatingly aware of two things: the absolute general ring of confidence that enveloped the braying hubbub (and my entire subsequent year) like a mist, and the fact that so many Freshers seemed to already know each other. Ready-mix friendships from hothouse schools, unlike mine, a despondent place of wearied teachers that pantingly squeezed out one, perhaps two, Trinity candidates per year. Hence my belly full of alcohol. It was going to liberate me, let me unfurl the mighty wings of banter latent within me, and fly me into the centre of it all, where I would be crowned the High King of Craic. The thought was sundered by the shock of finding the college strangely quiet. The front gate locked. What was up? Why … I asked myself … was Trinity closed? I asked a passerby.

'Is Trinity closed?'

'Trinity? That's the Custom House, ya muppet.'

Undeterred by this humiliating rebuke from a stranger, which would have had my still-sensitive teenage soul retire to my bed shivering in self-abnegation were I not fully tanked, I found my way onto campus, across its drizzled cobbles and into that strange, vaulted and windowless hobbit-hole of a bar, The Buttery. Excited by the activity and noise, and the perpetual pang of youthful horniness, I weaved from group to group, imposing myself loudly on everyone I encountered, talking what my father would viciously designate 'utter scutter' to faces in various rictuses of laughter and recoil. I have a final memory of that first horrific night, succeeding the rebuke at the Custom House on the ineradicable memory frieze. To a surprised guy in a Tommy Hilfiger sweater, I foamed (and I remember the exact words) that 'you are a middle-income aspirational shithead from Ranelagh who wishes he was British'. A bouncer's fingers rested on my shoulder.

It is accepted that the young attend third-level education to study a discipline. Throughout my first year, this fact fluttered nebulously around my experiences like the most delicate net curtain. Every now and again the curtain tightened, and I'd find myself in a lecture theatre actually attending to words, invariably around the discipline of Neuroscience. Images of the brain abounded, with little patches lit. Yellow. Red. Purple. This is your ambition. This is your fear. This is your fondness. This is your addiction.

'Neuroscience … is reductive horseshit,' I told my new friend, Bean, in the sticky chaotic depths of The Buttery hours later, as little patches of my own brain reduced in direct proportion to my student grant.

Yes, against all odds, I had made a friend. Having graduated from Eton, he was one of those bohemian English types who wafted around the Arts Block smelling of rolled up cigarettes, wool and patchouli-adjacent fragrance. Emergent from what I had begun to call my 'blippy blobby brain bullshit' lectures, I would watch them congregate outside the greener pastures of the Ussher Library, where the canon of English literature – the course I would have chosen had I not buckled under various external pressures – resided like the dragon's hoard in *Beowulf*. Bean was very posh, incredibly beautiful, exceptionally rich and transcendentally cool. Yet he had one remarkable aspect that drew us together like twinned stars – his name. Bean. It was a name that seemed to have evolved from nickname to perma-name, and it had been bestowed on him because, even as one considered his languid beauty, there was no escaping his being the spit of Mr Bean.

I too looked like Mr Bean. Bog Mr Bean as opposed to Hampstead Mr Bean, but Mr Bean all the same. Indeed, many of the most excruciating moments of my everyday life, during that endless era when that hapless man–child was a going concern on terrestrial television, involved completely random and often aggressive people calling me Mr Bean. The phenomenon was quite heightened, dramatic even, at times. A car once slowed down on O'Connell Bridge, almost causing a multiple-vehicle pileup, just so its driver could roar over the virile pulse of trance music pouring round his head, 'Yo, Mr Bean.' The fact that this tall, attractive dude, who had already been rated 9/10 in a notorious poll on a stall door in the Arts Block women's toilet, was getting the Mr Bean treatment to the point that it had become his actual name, soothed my heart in indescribable ways. In Rowan Atkinson resemblance terms, I had been out-Beaned by Bean. Yet he was charismatic, princely. He also liked the same music and drugs as me. In total, this was a rare and wonderful confluence of circumstance.

'Darragh, you're a man of local knowledge. I rather bet you know where the magical mushrooms grow,' he said to me one brisk and bleary morning at the start of November.

We were stood outside House 6 under a sky as cold and bright as toilet porcelain. He was flanked by his beautiful posh friends, Tara and Sam, who watched me quizzically from nests of tweed and wool. There was something detached about all three of them. It worried me because, mere weeks in, my friendship with Bean felt marked by a growing detachment on his part. I imagined the attraction of me thinning in his mind, like I was the human equivalent of last season's coat. My heart tightened at the prospect at not being able to satisfy him or the two exotic creatures by his side who all saw me as their 'local connection'. The season was long over. The hills frost-flecked and bare. And yet …

'They're long gone, lads,' I said, watching their faces drop while savouring anticipation of the effects wrought by the forthcoming wretched lie, 'but I can sort yiz out. I've a supply.'

I did not. My friend Ferdia did. A treasured brown jiffy bag secreted among dusty, decades-old pictures of saints atop a bockety teal wardrobe in one of those dilapidated Georgian bedrooms where indoor ice was a not-impossible prospect in the slicing cold of a January morning. He had gathered them on the slopes of the Sugar Loaf mountain across two days during that time when the fading sun causes them to prick into sudden existence like tiny, pale stars in the darkening flora. An effect that could be enhanced, according to Ferdia, by consuming 'no less than five and no more than ten of them' so that one's eyesight vibrates in affinity with the fungus and 'makes it glow'.

Later that week, I experienced an evening that emerges from the wet turmoil of the year like a serene island, a long-planned visit to Ferdia's to enjoy a potluck dinner with him and varied friends of his from a Dublin I did not know – a more quietly arty Dublin, peopled by the modestly idiosyncratic. Under blushed light, we ended the meal with homemade lemon drizzle cake and laughed into the small hours about strange subjects such as what tree wood made the best perfume. As soft music tapered into the squeak of a bike being wheeled through a door opening on the deep urban night, I caught a glimpse of a plane of existence a million miles away from my lived chaos, the dancing puppet I was constructing of myself to draw detached smiles from people whose grandparents might have seen me as an ape.

That night, as small, delicate Ferdia slept deeply on his couch, I did something despicable. I crept upstairs to rob half of his mushrooms. I had promised to wash his dishes. I did not even do that. The lad who months prior had been dumped like a bag of potatoes onto Front Square's cold cobbles for calling out wannabe Brits, drifted out the door like a lonely shade, his head filling with sad fantasies of languorously enunciated platitudes and cheek kisses, the stolen quarry stashed awkwardly in his pocket.

One of maybe two classic experiments in psychology I remember from my first year was a longitudinal study in delayed gratification – the Stanford Marshmallow Experiment. In this experiment a child is left alone in a room with a marshmallow for fifteen minutes. The child is instructed that they can eat the marshmallow if they want. However, if they hold out for fifteen minutes, they will get a second marshmallow. The marshmallow gobblers and marshmallow delayers were subsequently tracked through life, and it was found that the delayers enjoyed no end of success over the gobblers – higher test scores, job promotions, satisfaction with life. I hardly need to spell out why that experiment fascinated me on such a primal level. In all the novels, plays and films I had consumed up to that point in my life, I had identified with characters of intricately sketched psychology, but I doubt there is even one that caused such a violent shock of recognition as the child who gobbled the marshmallow. Indeed, had I had taken part in the experiment, I was convinced I would have formed a crazy outlier. The fastest gobbler. Sitting in my plastic highchair for the next fourteen minutes and fifty-nine and a half seconds, tearfully chastizing myself for gobbling, and wishing I had another chance, where I'd no doubt wait like a good boy for the treat doubled. As with marshmallows, so with mushrooms.

Throughout the morning, I peeped into the Jiffy bag at the tangled ball of dried fungus. I convinced myself that they were about to turn, to lose their potency. Moment on moment they seemed to shrink and even grow sad. Yes, the famous animism of the mushroom, activated on the first trip and switched on forever more. *You will have to eat us soon Darragh*, they communicated in that profound and silent language of psychedelic plants. *Eat us or else our secrets will dry, and you will never, ever know.* It was a Thursday, and the only lecture I had was in Behavioural Psychology, that notorious field that was begun by a man who put his daughter inside a box for a few hours a day on account of his successfully altering the behaviours of pigeons and rats in smaller boxes. Fuck boxes, I thought. It was an excellent day to break boxes to smithereens, to release rats, pigeons and unfortunate daughters into the laughing universe.

Furthermore, an afternoon society event was to follow the lecture, organized by the School of Drama society, the Players. All the louche scarf-wearers would be there. Bean and the entire gang. I mean, how cool would it be to arrive high and dole out the remainder of the mushrooms like a psychedelic trickster? Filled with euphoric resolve, I flung a Goodfellas Deep Pan pepperoni pizza into the encrusted black maw of our dying oven. Fifteen minutes after that, in great gulps that would shame a pelican, I drank cooling Linden Village cider to relieve the roof of my mouth. It was burnt to shreds by magically seasoned pizza.

One can led to two others, and the thought that the mushrooms were slow to work. So I scrunched a good few more up into clots and choked them down with acrid apple and stood up.

'Woops,' I said.

There was too much fuel in the engine. I immediately knew it. On the periphery of my vision, a blue plastic bag exhaled, gently, giving the barest intimation of being a human lung. By the time I contended with my duffel coat, I felt my leg bones gently soften. Progressively – gently, too – and one by one, things in the environment began to wake up and breathe. The early warning system of a Herculean trip abounded all around me. If I hadn't had the cider, I'd have done the only sane thing and hidden under a blanket for the following ten hours. Instead, I chose to spend them on-campus.

Skinner's daughter remained in her box because her would-be saviour, the psychedelic jester from the bog, got waylaid by the sight of his own fingers. I sat in the wet grass at the edge of the cricket pitch turning my hands palm up, palm down, marvelling at how my fingers morphed from meat to vegetation and back again, from dripping sausages one minute, to twisting purple twigs the next.

With my beige corduroy trousers clinging wetly to my thighs, I stumbled off in search of warmth, vaguely aware that I looked for all the world as if I had pissed myself. I followed a faint, magnetic tug, a recollection from what felt like a previous aeon that there was an event on somewhere and that the event, like so many subsequent events, would be filled with uncanny angel people. I was convinced that they would vibe on the love bubbling within me, return it and take me into their world of secrets and doors. I wandered through puddles of light that splashed around my feet. I became detached from the endless, teeming whimsy that was anywhere I might have cared to look. My vision turned inwards and my feet, like smooth machinery, carried me to the windowless, vaulted bar, a place that would effectively serve as a spiritual prison during the years that followed. Dreaming the clown's dream of being a king, a legend, at the centre of it all, I drowned the squirming world one glass after another. Soon there was nothing left, except my young voice babbling harsh nonsense to a hail of half-lit faces. I had a long way left to go.

Darragh McCausland (TCD 2000–4; Psychology) is a writer from Kells, Co. Meath. He has had short fiction and essays published in **The Dublin Review, Gorse, Stonecutter, The Tangerine** and **Lighthouse**. He is finishing a collection of short stories and a collection of essays.

TWO LITTLE BOYS

wayne jordan

WE MET doing a play in Players.

He was a crusader and I was a spear carrier. The play was complicated and full of passion and cruelty. We did English accents. A tall girl who wore skirts over her jeans directed. Audiences suffered it. Some friends of mine from school came and were polite. We were children playing at being soldiers. I had a key moment where I screamed about the brutalities we had inflicted and endured in the Holy Land. I assumed regular people just didn't 'get' the script. Not how I did. Not how we did. The conversations we all had about it. We were clearly plugged into greatness.

On the second to last night, I tied up his shoes for him before he went on stage. The laces wrapped around his calves after a medieval fashion. He sat on a bench and I knelt at his feet.

On the closing night, we had dinner in a pizza place on George's Street, the whole cast, after the show. I arrived a little late and he had kept a place for me beside him.

He was older than me. Three years. It would mean nothing now, but back then it gave his approval a monumental quality. And he was middle-class, or something like that. He was from the south side, his parents had been to university, they'd lived in Europe, spent the summers outside Dublin, down south on the sea. I adored him. The books he'd read.

I made some joke using a spoon as a prop and he got involved, joining in the performance, the two of us digging away at the restaurant wall with teaspoons. Everyone was laughing. It was a golden moment.

I felt his leg against mine under the table and I was aware that I was made up of a million, million molecules, because every one of them was fizzing and the space between them was honey.

At a house party that night, or a few nights later, we were sat on a sofa in the back room, he and I and someone else who quickly excused themselves. His arm was resting across the back of the couch and I leaned in and our lips met.

I had kissed some boys before. Someone at school. A boy from Liechtenstein in the basement of Eamonn Doran's. Some laddish chap who knocked around in the Phil or the Hist who admired my dungarees. A friend of a friend at a twenty-first. A chef from the restaurant I worked in. Nothing that amounted to much.

But there was something legit about this kiss. This wasn't a rehearsal.

His lips were pillowy and a bit dry and that was lovely. I didn't smoke then and he did and I was excited by the taste of booze and cigarettes off his mouth, which seemed so grown up and so illicit, like I'd just jumped a couple levels in the game of life.

His chin had a rime of lovely stubble on it.

We made out half the night and into the early morning. The taste of him. The texture of his tongue.

We made a little camp of love in the back room of that party across two chairs. Other people were sleeping on the couches and in other beds, in other parts of the house. I had so much desire for him.

He told me to slow down, that we would have plenty of time.

I played with the hairs on his chest in the morning. A matt of chestnut fur. It arranged itself in delicious swirls. There was something baroque about it, decorative, and the treasure trail from his chest to down below his belt.

His body was more compact than mine, which was longer and leaner, a little softer. His was tighter, stronger, more developed. His ribs were steel, his skin was hot. I studied the geography of his torso intently.

We walked to a bus stop together and parted shyly.

We went for a drink in Doyle's a few nights later, and he asked to be my boyfriend. We talked about theatre and identity and movies and politics and theory and style. It was dizzying.

I felt like I'd won a prize.

A friend we had in common would sing 'love is in the air' whenever he saw us after that.

We were a regular sight on the corridors and balconies of the Beckett Centre – canoodling, leaning, chatting, sighing – rapt.

People were sweet to us. And fond. We had good friends, and everyone was our friend.

It felt like the whole kind world doted on our romance. It was a time of 'coming out' and declaring 'pride' and helping people along with the idea of two boys or two girls together. We felt like soldiers of love. The new poets of desire. We were a beacon.

I loved holding his hand. He loved that I rubbed my eyes when I was sleepy.

The second or third time we were together was in some other friend's apartment on a pull-out bed. As we pawed each other's clothes off, I noticed that we had the same underwear on. They were unusual. Black with a blue strip on the side and white piping. I took that as a sign. When we were getting heavy in the dark, I became suddenly alarmed by the amount of fluid that was being generated so I turned on the lights. My nose was bleeding. He was kind and understanding, and I went to the bathroom to clean myself up. When I came back, he was sitting there with a sympathetic grin on his face, but, as he pulled back the covers to invite me back in, he revealed what he hadn't noticed but I did immediately. There was blood all over his body and all over his crotch. It looked like a crime scene. He washed off and was a bit distant, but it was only a matter of minutes before we got back on the horse. He was on top of me and kissing when he became still for a moment and the light went on again. He had a single thin line of blood coming from his own nose this time. A sympathetic nosebleed to match his sympathetic underpants. I took that, too, as a sign.

Our sex seems so chaste and naïve in hindsight. We both lived with our parents, and it was hard to get a run at it. Kissing and blowjobs, a bit of frottage and some early experiments towards a more advanced practice of lovemaking. But it made me feel beautiful and invincible. Like I was made of light.

I gave up chapel choir to spend more time with him. He, and not my father, taught me how to shave. We got in trouble in the Front Lounge for heavy petting in the afternoon. We had nowhere else to go, so we found nooks and crannies all over college to cradle in – the dressing rooms in the drama buildings, the disabled toilets in the Art's Block, unused corridors, the shadowy side of new science buildings, the rose garden, under a bush by the rugby pitch.

I stayed with him in his grandmother's house on Synge Street when she was away for a week. I learned to drink whiskey and cider, and he would make us pasta and sauce whenever we came in drunk. He read to me from the letters of famous Frenchmen and the novels of James Baldwin. His father dropped something over one afternoon and he made me hide in the bedroom.

I went to the Trinity Ball in a purple suit I borrowed from the costume basement, and I had a cream-coloured, ruffle-bibbed tuxedo shirt I wore with it. I drank some vodka from the bottle before I got the 29A to town. I was still a teenager.

He was waiting for me at the top of Grafton Street. He was in a tux and he looked like Steve McQueen.

At a party on a rooftop after, some posh girl made a remark about my clothes and he came to the rescue, though I wasn't bothered. But I was glad to have a hero. We went back someplace and made puppy love. Home was each other and all our friends and this great experiment.

We said I love you to each other and after that I couldn't stop. I terrified him. I terrified myself.

I love you I love you I love you I love you.

I became jealous and suspicious and afraid.

He wanted to take drugs and, at that time, that scared me.

He wanted to go places I wasn't ready to go.

I wanted to box up the world and us and everything, how we looked at each other, how everyone looked at us, and just pack it away, stop it from moving, from changing, from fading away. I wanted to strangle what we had so that I could keep it. And that's what I did, though that's not what happened.

For my birthday, he got me tickets to see Nina Simone in concert and a book called *The Bone People*. On the inside page, in a childish scrawl, he wrote something like – 'To Wayne, Happy Birthday, You're deadly, Love X.' We ate in an Italian place off Meeting House Square.

He couldn't come to the concert. I went with a friend. Nina sang 'Pirate Jenny' from *The Threepenny Opera* and the whole world shook. She had a golden dress and a golden fan.

'There's a ship/ The Black Freighter/ With a skull on its masthead/ Will be coming in ...'

That night he slept with someone else, or two people. Something modern and painful like that.

He told me about it soon after, and we had to break up.

At first I was understanding and philosophical, but that didn't last for long.

Then came the wailing and drinking and the fingernails down my face. I cornered any poor sinner who would listen to me. My eyes circled in their sockets. Sometimes I banged my head against walls. I was a scandal.

I roped people into this drama with a certain charm and intensity and an exquisitely arranged language of agony. I treated everyone as an audience.

He was still trying to be my friend, and so I tried to kill him with my hands or a knife at a party. I don't remember. I was blind drunk and devastated. I know I was pulled off him. That was not a golden moment.

I went to the doctor in Donaghmede. I borrowed money from my father. I told him I was in pain and I couldn't sleep/breathe/concentrate/eat. He was quiet and compassionate and told me I was heartbroken. He said that in time things would be okay, and he prescribed me some B12 tablets.

I listened to Nina Simone on repeat:

'I get along without you very well/ ... Except when soft rains fall ...' I went to some hatchet-faced college counsellor with thick glasses and a dyed-scarlet bob. A silk scarf with a print hanging off her shoulder. She told me I needed to own my pain.

This was both true and not true. I was out of control. But it strikes me, still, as a measly response to the size and provenance of my trauma.

I was suffering a major attack of something like PTSD, ignited by this breakup and his rejection, sure, but caused by years of brutal and violent conditioning at the hands of the quasi-fascist Catholic state apparatus that operated divisive hierarchies of sexual shame, and that despised and stigmatized my nature … This was the kind of thing I would go on to learn to articulate at Trinity.

The range of options that had seemed available to me as a young person (to all of us around) could only be described as meagre. A black and white existence with rare flashes of colour drawn from intoxication or the imagination.

But at the turn of the millennium, I had stood on the precipice of happiness, a full-bodied, full-blooded fire of possibility, and nothing had prepared me for having something to lose. So, for a little while, I went crazy. Which I think is fair enough.

I did well at college. Got a scholarship. Tried a PhD.

Became friends with him, eventually. He had troubles of his own.

I'm glad I knew him in the way I did when we were young. He was my Romeo, my Heathcliff. And not everyone gets one of those.

He set me alight. My mind and body.

And that was only a beginning

I never read *The Bone People*.

You're deadly, Love X.

Photo credit: Traolach Ó Buachalla.

Wayne Jordan (TCD 1998–2002, Drama and Theatre Studies; 2004–6, MLitt/PhD) is a theatre artist and director. During his studies at the Samuel Beckett Centre from 2004–6, he took a year off books to pursue work as a theatre director and never returned. He has worked extensively at the Gate and Abbey Theatres and his work has toured throughout Ireland and the UK. He lived in Prague for the last three years, studying and making work at a school for experimental theatre and puppetry. Wayne has now returned to Ireland, where he teaches at The Lir National Academy of Dramatic Art at Trinity College Dublin.

CONFESSIONS OF A NERD AND OTHER STORIES

claire hennessy

FROM MY mid-teens onwards, I was convinced I wanted to be a counselling psychologist and it was only partly to do with Deanna Troi on *Star Trek: The Next Generation*, because not only did she get to be a counsellor but she got to do it in space. While eating chocolate-fudge sundaes yet still looking slim. It really was a utopian future presented in that show.

The summer I was fifteen, because I was the sort of nerdy kid that spent three weeks of every summer at an academic programme for high-ability students, I took a course in psychology and, like most intense young humans, felt I'd found my calling. Crucially, it was a more practical calling than this creative writing business, which I had discovered in my early teens did not necessarily involve as much money as one might expect. (My first novel for teenagers was published when I was thirteen, although *almost* fourteen. A fellow writer once told me: 'Jesus, when I was thirteen I was discovering masturbation,' and I remain unsure which of us got the better deal there.) (But, well: her.)

Recently a friend of mine began explaining how Second Year Arts places were allocated for psychology students in UCD back in the day, and I had to stop her and explain that these details were still tattooed onto my brain. I had carefully, diligently, researched my options. In those days it was a Master's, rather than a doctorate, in counselling psychology that one undertook, though it was still a demanding programme. I had a plan, like a proper mature adult, or the Cylons in *Battlestar Galactica*.

Then I got into Trinity as a psychology student, and every time I set foot on campus it got a tiny bit harder to breathe.

It was not an entirely smooth process, getting in. In a truly delicious memory of irony, my Leaving Cert maths exam (higher-level, even!) had been added up incorrectly; a quick re-check (rather than the longer process of re-marking) brought me up a grade just in time to start the term at Trinity, having spent a week at UCD. (I do understand it is the done thing to pretend that Trinity is a posher institution, but after two days out in Belfield I could hear my voice going pure Ross O'Carroll-Kelly.)

So I knew I was supposed to feel lucky. And I did. And then I didn't.

There were two things you were supposed to know, if you were going to study psychology in an academic setting. The first was that you couldn't escape maths – statistics was a huge part of it all. This intimidated and terrified many people, apparently. The second was that psychology was not your personal path to understand yourself better. It was not going to be like therapy.

I went in knowing this. I was as prepared as any eighteen-year-old could be. I – this is kind of embarrassing – quite enjoyed the statistics bits of things.

I don't know why I say embarrassing. It's kind of awesome, actually. The looming monster of doom that we were all expected to be terrified of was something I found manageable. Did you know that it's possible to get more than 70 on an assignment or test in Trinity? More than 80? Magic!

I sometimes have clever reasons for why psychology was not right for me then, in that particular institution, and I think there's some validity to it. Lab reports, of which there were many, felt like busywork; an insistence on how psychology was a totally valid science (please fund our neuroscience programme!) led to the use of quantitative methods where qualitative methods might have been more useful. The requirement to participate in a certain amount of postgraduate students' research – common in many psychology programmes – felt more interesting than intrusive, but has left me with a slight eye-rolling tendency every time I hear about studies conducted on university campuses. I also still occasionally twitch at that one where I had to generate sufficient saliva to fill a test tube.

But all of this might be simply an attempt at intellectualizing the common human dilemma: I have made a mistake. Shit. What do I do?

Repeating a year, transferring course or 'dropping out' – the last term being one I sometimes used to make myself feel, like, cool and edgy – are not terribly unusual things for students to encounter, though I suspect harder now than they used to be. (Tuition fees at Trinity are currently slightly lower than they were in the noughts, €2681 in 2020/21 in comparison to three and a half grand back then – which sounds like a bargain until you remember that the 'student contribution fee', which used to be almost nominal, is set at 3k.) When you're nineteen, you're still young enough to feel like a year is a vast stretch of time.

You're still stupid enough to feel superior when, in your intro lecture for English Literature students, some poor soul puts up her hand and asks about how things are different from Leaving Cert English and you just want to *die of embarrassment* on her behalf. This is *university*, like.

Aside from this minor drama, which did not feel minor at the time, I loved my undergraduate degree. I paired up English with History, because having another subject rather than doing pure English was the way of avoiding the apparent nightmare Old English, and I sank into all the reading and the analysing of texts.

I was grateful to be there, without imagining it to be perfect. People sometimes speak of academia as an ivory tower as though other areas of work don't have their faults and their insularities, as though it's not a difficult space that demands serious work. I learned how to value hard work in Trinity. There may well be subjects where things simply 'click' for people, but for the arts and humanities there's no way around devoting substantial time to whatever it is you're writing about or researching. (There may well be a way, but don't tell me, I'll cry.)

For many 'bright' kids, there's a mismatch between the skills you need to develop to learn stuff, and the actual learning of that stuff. What I mean is, if there's things you already know – if you, say, have memorized your seven-times-tables before it comes up in school – or topics you just 'get', you don't go through the process of learning-how-to-learn alongside learning-the-material in the way that the system has intended. And while that's pretty darn handy, at some point everyone hits a wall. And many people don't get past it. (Did I mention that I ended up going back to work on that academic programme for high-ability kids? I'll get off the soapbox now.)

In my Senior Freshman year (god, Trinity, why can't you just be *normal* and call it Second Year?) I basically lived in the library, studying like a fiend and trying not to despair about how I was not an effortless genius. I wanted the stamp of approval the college offers, and then maybe I would feel like a legitimate clever human. You know the one I mean.

If one gets Schol, or Schols, or however one abbreviates the scholarship yoke, you are entitled to use the letters 'Sch.' after your name.

It is a truth universally acknowledged that actually doing so makes you a bit of a wanker.

And that's pretty much all I've got on the social side of what the whole thing means. It's a weird old business. There's an oath in Latin that I'm fairly sure involves having to throw yourself in front of the Provost if there's a bullet coming his way.

I did in my time certainly encounter people who felt that Commons, the evening meal in the Dining Hall – open to everyone but with the fee covered for Scholars and Fellows of the College (and yes all of these things must be in Capital Letters) – was this vital chance for the cream of the crop to have deep philosophical chats about things and to network and do all that kind of shit.

Please see above re: wankery.

I honestly don't have a clue how widespread this idea was, or is. I almost never went to Commons during the time I was eligible, partly because I found it intimidating and stressful and partly because I often worked in the evenings.

The presumption is, as with many other things in Trinity (hello, here is your timetable ten seconds before 9 am on Monday of week one of term), that students have no other commitments. And as a human who passionately believes in education, I would love to see that be the case. There are benefits to working alongside studying, but a degree (even an Arts degree)* is a demanding thing. There are benefits to adequate sleep, too.

---

* Okay, maybe 'even an Arts degree if you want a decent grade'. I might occasionally lapse into idealism, but I'm not totally delusional.

I loved the learning, though. I mean, I loved the learning so much I returned to Trinity the following decade for two postgraduate degrees (see: actual non-status reasons for trying to get Schols), and I swear at least 90 per cent of that was geeky enthusiasm and only 5 per cent was a kind of Stockholm Syndrome.

I learned about Judith Butler and gender-as-performative before it was all on Tumblr, mostly via the incredible queerness of Charlotte Brontë's *Villette*.

I was riveted by Darryl Jones's lecture (no, not the notorious twenty-seven-stages-of-decomposition-of-a-human-corpse one) on *The Da Vinci Code*. This was how you took all this analysis stuff and applied it to the books or other media people were currently feverishly consuming. This was – a legitimate thing.

I justified spending an entire day in the library reading *The Nun* by Denis Diderot because it had been discussed, briefly, in Joseph Clarke's course on the cultural history of Europe in the eighteenth and nineteenth centuries. Fictional lesbian shenanigans in a convent, I reassured myself, would totally be a thing one could write about in the exam. (They were not. I also feel like I should take this moment to hope that the professor in question, who ended up supervising my History dissertation, does not still have nightmares about me putting up my hand and chirping, 'So, there's this cross-dressing lady warrior who I think really offers interesting insights into gender during the French Revolution,' or 'So, there were these places the gay men hung out in pre-revolutionary Paris,' or 'So, menstrual disorders in the eighteenth century.')

I read Mary Hays's *Memoirs of Emma Courtney*, which features this line written from a man to a woman: 'Your narrative leaves me full of admiration for your qualities, and compassion for your insanity.' It has stayed with me.

I understood almost nothing about critical theory when it was first taught to me (First Year English) or taught to me again (Third Year History) but figured out Marxist theory in time to be able to discuss *Hamlet* with reference to *The Lion King* and *Blackadder*.

I discovered that the wildly nationalistic way in which Irish history had been taught in primary and secondary school might benefit from some nuance. (But this is not a thing to bring up on nights out.)

I gave a presentation on *The Memoirs of Mrs Leeson* for David Dickson's seminar on Georgian Dublin, because who doesn't love eighteenth-century brothel-keepers?

I wrote essays on Oscar Wilde, on *Frankenstein*, on schoolgirl honour in Enid Blyton's series fiction. On witches and medieval French kings and Anastasia imposters and Marian apparitions.

I read so many books, so many articles, so many things.

None of it is ever enough. Nothing will ever quite make you feel smart enough or good enough. But I am still aware it's not nuthin' to have a Trinity degree in your back pocket, or to have the shiny extras: a first, a gold medal. It's always easy to say something is no big deal when it's about something you have.

There are gaps in my college story. I was bad at making friends on my course, even though I had friends (she said desperately, hoping to reassure). I didn't do many – any – of the things that you might expect a writer-type to do: join the Literary Society, leap into debating, start writing for one of the campus newspapers. I went to a couple of balls, but never the Trinity Ball. While I don't regret this, I do sometimes find myself around other graduates who think we speak a common language and yearn for a dictionary. (What Trinity did *they* go to?)

I did not leave Trinity as a counselling psychologist, as per the original plan. But I did leave after having been through my first round of counselling, via the services in the college. (Do you see how I've brought this around, all circle-like? Can I have a gold star?)

The bout of glumness that hit me in my first year there, with the wrong-course-not-belonging-oh-dear feeling, was not the first time I'd felt such things. By a long shot. I suspected it went beyond typical life-angst, while also fearing that it didn't. Maybe things were just this hard for everyone, and I was weak/terrible/stupid/etc.

One of the promises I made to myself, embarking on the new, shiny degree, was that if the sads hit badly again, I was off to seek help – not least because it was free and therefore this wasn't so much self-indulgent as it was frugal.

And I did.

The details are fairly boring because chronic depression is fairly boring. It feels like you're a bratty teenager not appreciating the good things in your life, like you are a whiny, spoiled child, like you are just crap at coping and then also like you want to throw yourself into the sea (but not the Liffey because you have standards oh OK maybe the Liffey oh dear lord what's happening).

It's melodramatic and tiresome. I imagine it is frustrating for Science students because it so often makes no sense; it's so irrational. And for Arts/Humanities students it is often romanticized, which – I mean, spare me. You're not feckin' Goethe.

Anyway, the point is, counselling helped a bit. It was not a fix, and it's often not appropriate to imagine that it might be, but it helped.

And that's the other kind of learning I did during my undergrad years. You don't get a certificate for it. But it happens.

A certificate would be kind of cool, though.

Claire Hennessy (TCD 2009, History and English Literature; MPhil Popular Literature; MPhil Creative Writing) is a writer, editor, book reviewer and creative writing facilitator based in Dublin. She has published twelve novels for young adults as well as short fiction and poetry. She is the co-founder and co-director of Dublin's online creative writing school the Big Smoke Writing Factory, and co-founder and co-editor at **Banshee**, a literary journal and small press. After she graduated from Trinity in 2009, she returned the following decade for postgraduate courses in Popular Literature and Creative Writing.

ADVENTURE OF THE UNKNOWN

uché gabriel akujobi

IT WAS one of those rare warm, sunny Dublin days and I had just finished a game of football with my team. I was in a good mood; we'd won. As soon as I got home, I logged into my computer to check my CAO application and see if I'd gained a place at what I considered the most prestigious university in Ireland, Trinity College. There were so many thoughts going through my mind as I waited for that page to load. Suddenly, the words appeared on the screen telling me I'd been accepted. I kept checking my application over and over again to make sure I was seeing it right. It wasn't a dream, it was real life and it felt unbelievable. That was a life-changing moment.

I had come into Ireland as an asylum seeker, and for a long time I never thought I would enter the four walls of an Irish university as one of its students. Back then, asylum seekers weren't eligible for a third-level education grant, and if you wanted to attend university you had to pay international fees. Fortunately, I was granted leave to remain just before sitting my Leaving Certificate exams, which meant I was at least eligible for EU fees. All I had to do now was to pass those final exams, which was one of the biggest challenges I had ever faced in my life.

I first learned about Trinity College at a study group organized by the local parish for migrant students which I was fortunate enough to be part of. There,

I was tutored by students from Trinity College while preparing for my Leaving Cert. I felt incredibly lucky to be getting one-on-one lessons in higher-level maths, deciphering old Shakespearean English in the form of *Macbeth* and of course some tantalizing physics. I was in awe of how intelligent my tutors were, their command of English and their general philosophy of life. I knew then that Trinity College was definitely my number one choice for university. To say I was elated when I realized I'd been accepted would not do it justice. I was over the moon.

I remember First Year Freshers' Week like it was yesterday because I had never experienced anything like it before. I had already begun my journey to becoming an actor, so DU Players – the college drama society – was my first port of call. I'd experienced being in the Players Theatre a year before – a drama student looking for actors for his presentation of Athol Fugard's apartheid-era play *The Island* somehow found me, and I convinced one of my friends to take part in an excerpt with me. It was a wonderful experience, and it felt surreal being on a college stage as a sixth-year student. It kind of gave me a glimpse of what the future could be, and I loved it. The people I met during the production were so nice, and I started to imagine myself becoming a Trinity student. I had also previously performed with a group of friends at one of the university's Afro-Caribbean society events as I sang and played the *djembe* (a West African hand drum). So, by the time Freshers' Week came, I already knew my way around a little bit.

Aside from Players, I also joined the Afro-Caribbean society, and that was when my Trinity life began in earnest. There weren't many members in the society, but the sound of their drums on Front Square during Freshers' Week made up for it. It was reassuring to see more people like me, plus they were celebrating my culture. I belonged there, it felt like a no-brainer to join the society. Having played with them before, I had arrived in Trinity knowing I wanted to be part of this group of musicians. I had gotten to know the president from my previous performance, and he insisted that I take over the *djembe* drumming workshops. He somehow knew I was good at teaching before I realized I had a knack for it. It was a new experience, but I always relished a challenge. In my first year as the drumming instructor, I managed to get all the students to take part in the St Patrick's Festival Parade. To our surprise, we won first prize in the parade and subsequently received loads of requests to perform at various events. As luck/destiny would have it, I ended up being the *djembe* drumming teacher for the rest of my time in Trinity.

I met so many people during my first year alone that it felt like I'd made enough friends and had no room for anyone else. Little did I know how important those friendships would become when trying to survive loneliness and boredom throughout my time at Trinity. Before then, the only people I really knew were those I'd met while living in Direct Provision. I came to Ireland seeking asylum aged fifteen and spent the following three years living in that hostel. Two years in, I received a deportation letter and spent a whole year fighting it. That was a really taxing period in my life – being told there was a one-way flight waiting to take me back to Nigeria. Fortunately, a lot of people rallied around me and lobbied on my behalf – my school, my theatre group, various community groups I was part of, my church, my friends. They were successful, and the order was overturned. After all that, being able to mix with students, integrate, whatever you want to call it, made me feel so alive.

As a member of the Players society, I took part in their Freshers' play known as *The Co-Op*. It was a fun, crazy and quite intense experience where you spent a lot of time with people you'd just met. If you were lucky, you got to call some of them your friends. I was used to being outside my comfort zone, so it didn't feel hard to blend in. Plus, I was acting, and I was good at it. However, it was difficult to make proper friends, as I was working part-time and couldn't join the cast when they went out drinking and partying after rehearsals. In the end, I only made one real friend who I hung out with for the rest of my time at uni.

I'd decided to study Business Economics and Social Studies, or BESS as it was known among students. My first year was all right, I suppose. I was the only African at that time in a class of about eighty students. I stood out, of course. However, I was never one to shy away from a challenge, and I found my acting experience helped me deal with a lot of the pressure. As an actor, I believe you have a stronger sense of yourself and are able to adapt to any situation you find yourself in. It helped me communicate easily in a group, and I never shied away from speaking up.

But making friends in that class was hard. It felt as if everyone was stuck up or just didn't know how to approach me. I remember meeting a few people at one of our class social gatherings, and the next day they completely blanked me like we had never met. This happened on numerous occasions, right up until I graduated. It felt like I didn't have much in common with my classmates other than the fact that we were studying the same course. I honestly wasn't sure how they saw me – sometimes I thought they felt I was stupid. When I tried to make an effort to find out about them, they didn't want to know anything about me. It made me feel invisible.

The friends I ended up making were students from abroad, other courses and the societies I joined. I was drawn to those from other countries because we all felt the same – we were in a foreign place and had to band together to survive. I realized it was much harder than I originally anticipated to make true friends at university and to feel accepted, especially since my story was so different to the average student's.

It was like my college friends and I were from two different worlds. They could travel all over Europe on a whim while I had to always apply for a visa. I needed a month's notice to send in my visa application, save money for the visa and also find the cash for the tickets. This made it hard to bond with the young people around me. I didn't want to explain my complicated situation whenever someone asked me to go abroad with them. Maybe if I had been upfront with them, things might have turned out differently. Maybe I would have been accepted, maybe I would have made long-lasting friends – I guess I'll never know.

In my second year, I moved to Trinity Halls accommodation in Rathmines and became President of the Trinity Afro-Caribbean Society. It was a busy year and I had to learn the ropes quickly. Administrative duties were never my strong point – honestly, they still aren't – but I played my part. I was still teaching the *djembe* drumming classes and also had to coordinate other instructors.

As a result, I started falling behind in class but knew that I could always catch up. Second Year BESS was slightly better. Another African student who had to repeat a year joined my class and, naturally, we clicked. He was originally from Nigeria, so it was easy for us to understand each other. I still found a lot of my conversations with classmates superficial. It had become clear that most of them either knew each other prior to coming to Trinity College or had some sort of connection I was unaware of. I tried my best to fit in, but it just didn't work.

I had first heard about Trinity Ball during my first year but couldn't afford to go. In Second Year, I was going. I saved up the money for a ticket and made plans with a few friends for the day. I dressed up in my finest tux. Well, my only tux that I had also saved up for.

I met some mates for drinks before going for dinner at a restaurant on Harcourt Street. At one point during the meal, I decided I needed to go outside for air, as I was feeling quite drunk. Outside, I met a friend and we ended up having a very bizarre chat. That was my final memory of the night. The next day I woke up in my bed with my ball ticket unused in my pocket. My first attempt at attending Trinity Ball was clearly not a success, and I was quite upset that I'd missed the whole thing after all the effort I put in. From then on, I made a mental note never ever to drink on an empty stomach. I also haven't drunk red wine since that day.

Third Year was the best. I had matured a little bit and also met Erasmus students who I still keep in touch with today. It was during my third year I made a decision to go by my Nigerian name – Uché. It confused a lot of people, and I had to explain over and over again that in Nigeria you usually have two names, especially if you are a Christian or a Muslim. My Christian name is Gabriel. Everyone at college knew me by that name. But I needed to make a change to fully express myself as a human and as a student. So, I started introducing myself as Uché and it felt great. It made me feel more complete. Some people still called me Gabriel, as it was hard for them to switch. I just let them be.

When I first joined the Afro-Caribbean society, most of our members were Europeans but we started to see more African and Caribbean students joining up. I also stopped taking part in Players' events, as I had started acting professionally. I was part of Arambé productions, which was the only African theatre production company at that time and was doing a lot of interesting projects with them.

It was during my third year that I had to decide what I wanted out of my degree – I focused on accounting and business management, but it was difficult academically, as I was doing so many extra activities outside my studies. Luckily, my roommate, an Erasmus student from Germany, was brilliant at accounting and business management, so we studied together. I wasn't lonely this time – what a relief and a blessing. I learned a lot from him, as he was a year older and seemed to have had his future planned out. I had never really given much thought to a career as an accountant or in business. I was an actor and that was that. You're probably wondering why I studied BESS, of all things, if being an actor was all I wanted. A wise person had once advised me to have a back-up plan if I really wanted to act. Boy, were they right! But that's a tale for another time.

I spent most of my fourth and final year studying and rounding things up with the Afro-Caribbean society. I wanted to leave with a good degree and to be able to manage my own business as an actor. I also wanted to run a drumming school after graduation, so I was in the process of setting it up.

Now, more than a decade on, when I look back over my time at Trinity College, I realize it actually helped to shape me in a way that I've never really given it credit for. I had to learn to look after myself, and I also discovered first-hand what it meant to lead an organization, albeit through a college society. I met people who are still my friends today and others who briefly passed through my life but taught me valuable lessons. I honed my skills as a people person and as a leader – even though I never saw myself as one. It was indeed hard at times, but in the end having good friends made all the difference.

Uché Gabriel Akujobi (TCD 2006–10; Business, Economics and Social Studies) is an actor, director, musician and writer originally from Nigeria. During his thirteen years in Ireland he has been an active member of Discovery Gospel Choir, Trinity Afro-Caribbean Society and the Dún Laoghaire Refugee Project. His acting work includes **Butcher Babes** by Bisi Adigun, **The Kings of the Kilburn High Road** by Jimmy Murphy, **Strike** by Tracy Ryan and the award-winning documentary **Blood Fruit** by Sinead O'Brien. He has also appeared on RTÉ's **Fair City** and is a founding member of Yankari Afrobeat Collective.

IN WITH THE OLD

dylan haskins

I WENT TO Trinity because I was told to. In 2006, I had completed a Leaving Cert which, I thought at the time, was of little consequence. I'd already been offered a place to study Design in Visual Communications at IADT, based mainly on my portfolio of cut-and-paste punk fanzines, posters and photography. The Leaving Cert finished in late June. The summer started perfectly. Our DIY punk *Basta! Youth Collective* organized a tour of five bands playing shows all around Ireland, including my own folk–punk band *D!SKO TRA!TOR* – styled exactly like that. The final night of the tour was a house gig in a living room in Wexford. We uploaded the video of our band's set that night to the one-year-old, still relatively unknown, YouTube.

Back from the tour on a balmy summer Monday night, walking to a small house party in Shankill with a friend, I remember clocking how perfect that moment in time felt. A few hours later, my phone rang. It was my mum calling to say my dad had died. They came to pick me up in the car and brought me to his house in Deansgrange where an ambulance and Garda car were parked outside. My parents had been separated since I was two, but this was the first house I'd lived in. I remember leaning on that front wall, looking up at the house and thinking, 'I guess I'm an adult now.'

Dad lived there on his own after the separation. I'd spoken to him a few days before, and he told me he had a tummy bug and was going to sleep it off. But the phone rang out that weekend and, before heading to the house party, I asked my uncle to knock into the house. He was the one who had to kick the door in when there was no answer. One of the last weekends I'd spent with Dad, we'd been driving through Rathdrum in Wicklow, and he talked about how out of control the property market was. He said it would inevitably crash and people would be handing the keys to their overvalued houses back to banks.

I had lots of ideas of what art college would be like, and at the start it was such a novelty to be able to spend all day doing and making, and thinking creatively, without having to then break and go to 'real' subjects, as had been the case in school. I was elected class rep, the first and only time I'd win an election. I learned about screen-printing and typography. But very quickly Vis Comm at IADT began to feel like we were being trained to produce work in volume for commercial clients.

That same year, with a bit of guidance and encouragement from Willie White at Project Arts Centre, I'd applied for and been awarded funding from the Broadcasting Authority of Ireland to make a documentary film called *Roll Up Your Sleeves* about the DIY culture and ethos that underpinned our local punk scene. It included a budget to travel abroad for interviews. I asked IADT for a year out to focus on the film, but the request was refused. I was told I needed to focus on coursework rather than extracurricular activities. So I dropped out and made the film instead.

As the film production was wrapping up, I didn't really know to do next. I was still grieving but not really addressing it. My mum's parents could see I was at this loose end – dropping out of college, having just turned twenty-one and at an important life juncture, with an annual CAO deadline looming. They invited me for dinner one night with four of their old friends. It quickly became clear they had an ulterior motive. As I remember it, my grandmother took command of the conversation and suddenly made an announcement in front of everyone gathered for the meal. 'This is what you're going to do, Dylan,' she told me. 'You're going to go to Trinity. It doesn't matter what you study as long as you find it interesting, and you've at least one inspiring lecturer, because college isn't about what you learn, it's about teaching you how to think. And it's your web of friends for the future.' I don't remember much of the subsequent conversation, but I do know the night ended with my grandmother and I sitting up late, drinking wine. It was the last real time I spent with her, as she too died a month or two later.

My grandparents had both attended UCD, albeit when it was a much smaller campus in Earlsfort Terrace. Their thinking behind the recommendation to go to Trinity wasn't borne of nostalgia – but of the practicalities of scale. Trinity was smaller, and you could be part of a department where you actually knew everyone. I've always been independent and charted my own course, but equally my grandparents weren't the sort to dole out such specific and forceful advice. They'd had a much more laissez-faire attitude to their own four daughters' education. So, in those very particular circumstances, and considering how old they all were, I decided to take their advice.

I considered applying for something like history or philosophy, and asked some friends who were already in Trinity for their timetables so I could sit in and sample a few lectures. None of them did it for me. I remembered how once a week in IADT I'd loved Sheera Murphy's US West Coast-infused lectures in visual culture. Nothing quite so New Age was on offer in Trinity, but History of Art and Architecture seemed like the next best thing. I chose Ancient History and Archaeology as my second subject. Combined, it was a mouthful when people asked you what you were studying. That was probably part of the reason I swapped Ancient History for Classical Civilization in Second Year. That and the realization I didn't care as much about *how* we uncovered the past. I was more interested in what people did and why.

I'd chosen History of Art, without thinking there was a whole other half of the course dedicated to the history of architecture. But it was actually architectural history that would capture my interest most and remain a passion long after I left college. Learning to read buildings and decipher their evolution, ideas and references has meant I'm never bored sitting on the top deck of a bus or visiting a new place. Studying the art and architecture of a particular time and people can tell you so much more about what makes a society tick than is revealed by a simple historical narrative of events.

During my time making the documentary, I'd also set up a small, independent record label and released the debut album by the Irish band Heathers.

Early into Trinity's Michaelmas term, Heathers were invited to perform at an important industry showcase in New York. I requested a few days off to fly to New York with them. Given my previous experience with IADT, I wasn't expecting the response I got from Peter Cherry, head of Art History that year. He quizzed me about what I was doing, more out of intrigue than suspicion, before telling me it was fine and that 'there's more to life than just college, go do what you have to do'.

I couldn't believe the contrast in attitude. I'd partly chosen IADT on the logic that as a relatively new institute, it would be more liberal and progressive, but found the opposite from the course and department heads. I'd expected Trinity to be more stuck in its ways and conservative, but actually – from the Art History department, at least – there was a bigger-picture perspective. Maybe this came from the confidence of having students pass through the gates for 400-odd years and not feeling like the college had something to prove. Whatever the reason, it felt like an encouraging environment to be part of.

During the first three years at Trinity, I always felt like I'd one foot inside and one foot outside in the real world. In Second Year, I had a part-time job presenting a live TV show on RTÉ2. I mostly worked it around my timetable, but unfortunately missed all of my Power and Identity in Ancient Rome lectures on a Tuesday afternoon. Friends would sign me in every other week so it didn't look like I was a total no-show. That same year, I also ran the Trinity Arts Festival and with a bunch of NCAD students set up a collectively run arts space called Exchange Dublin in Temple Bar. Having a busy life outside of Trinity saved me getting totally wrapped up in a Trinity bubble, but by Final Year I did somewhat regret trying to do so much and not fully immersing myself in the finite and fleeting four-year undergrad experience.

My dad hadn't been wrong about mortgage defaults. Third Year began with the politically tumultuous autumn and winter of 2010. Writing from the vantage point of October 2020, what is it about the end of decades and the sense of the world imploding? On the evening of 21 November 2010, I was in the library late working on an essay when I started to see rumblings on Twitter about a major announcement and impromptu press conference by the government of Brian Cowen. As much to procrastinate the essay as to potentially witness an important moment in Irish history, I left my desk and walked around the corner to Government Buildings on Merrion Square.

It was a cold night, and two very distinct groups had gathered outside the gates of Leinster House: what seemed like all of the world's media and a handful of protestors. I managed to blag my way past the first security post, a skill I'd honed at music festivals, and got as far as the entrance foyer. The press conference was about to start, but I didn't know where. Another guard asked me to wait while he got someone to bring me to the room where the media were assembled. A man, clearly quite stressed, came running down the stairs, quizzed me on who had sent me, correctly judged I wasn't supposed to be there and sent me on my way. I later realized it was the government press secretary, who undoubtedly had better things to be doing at that moment. Within the hour, it was confirmed to the nation that the government had requested a bailout of at least €80 billion from the EU and IMF. It quickly became inevitable there would be a general election in early 2011.

Just over a month later, in the final days of the decade, my housemate Una Mullally pointed out there wasn't really any party we could wholeheartedly vote for, given the recent history. 'One of us has to run,' she told me. 'It'll have to be you.'

By early January, we were planning an election campaign and building a team. I was going to run as an independent candidate for the constituency of Dublin South East, which included Trinity College. As extracurricular activities go, this was probably pushing it. By the end of January, we'd launched a campaign, come up with a load of policies, secured endorsements from everyone from Panti to Diarmaid Ferriter and built a team of around 200 volunteers. None of the core group had been involved in national politics before – we were very much making it up as we went along. The campaign caught the attention of the media, which, because of the circumstances, also included media from outside Ireland. Evenings were spent canvassing homes and attending campaign events, with days dedicated to giving interviews to *The Guardian*, *The Financial Times*, *BBC Newsnight*, *Le Monde*, Deutsche Welle and Al Jazeera.

By the end of February, it was over. I did well for a first-time candidate, finishing ahead of Sinn Féin and some well-established independents, but I didn't get elected. I hadn't set foot in Trinity for the two months, and my absence was undoubtedly highlighted to all of my lecturers by the presence of a giant poster featuring my (very young-looking) face hanging on a lamppost outside the college's Nassau Street entrance.

Revising for my Classics finals that summer wasn't so much about revision as reading course notes for the first time and realizing what fascinating modules I'd missed. I honestly don't think I'd have passed had it not been for the discovery of the back catalogue of BBC Radio 4 *In Our Time* episodes. I sat some of the exams in the same RDS hall as had been used for the election count. I remember pausing in the middle of one exam and looking up at a balcony where just a couple of months earlier I'd been interviewed by Al Jazeera in front of their audience of millions, and thinking how bizarre the whole thing was.

For my final year, I wanted to put both feet firmly back inside campus. I've always been overly nostalgic. Losing my Dad made me even more aware of the transience of life, and I wanted to commit to the experience of doing just one thing and doing it well. I tried to breathe in every moment of that fourth year, almost imagining myself looking back on it from the future. I wrote a piece for *The Irish Times* about my last Trinity Ball, which concluded:

> We can always return as alumni, but this was our last ball as undergraduates. Never again would all of these familiar faces and friends be together like this. But the 53rd ball will always have been ours, even when the photos are faded to mementos of another time. You stay classy, Trinity.

How wanky and cringe. It wouldn't be the worst were it not for that last line. But it does capture how wrapped up in it all I'd become.

I wrote my dissertation on 'scale and identity in the architecture of the Arts Building'. Unloved as it is, it's actually a listed building but had never really been researched. I spent hours in the Manuscripts Reading Room, poring over memos from the architects and college authorities in the 1960s and 1970s. To get to that reading area, you had to walk through the Long Room of the Old Library, past the tourists and up the magnificent, slightly wonky 300-year-old oak staircase in the west pavilion.

As Fourth Year Art History students, we had access to the serene TRIARC reading rooms in the converted stables of the Provost's House. Geography

Fourth Years had the key to the library in the stunning Ruskin-inspired Museum Building. My friend Rachel Murray was one such key holder, so when the regular library was closing up, I would head over there for a bit more work and chats. I finished writing my dissertation in that library late one night while drinking some red wine being shared around. It was late, summer was approaching and we stood in the chilly, late-night stillness of the rose garden, sharing a cigarette even though none of us actually smoked.

My dad's mother came to my graduation with my mum and my sister. Unlike my mum's parents, who had both been to university, Nanny Haskins had grown up in Carlow in a house without electricity or running water. She had moved to Dublin as a teenager to work as a house servant and met her husband James as she 'stepped off the number eight bus and into his arms'. They married and had eight children, who she reared in a small council house in Glasthule. Despite living in Dublin for over seventy years, that November morning in 2012 was the first time she'd ever set foot on the Trinity cobblestones. I don't think I ever saw her cry, but she did get emotional in Front Square after the graduation ceremony. With a choke in her voice, she told me how she never thought she'd see the day 'one of ours would pass through here'.

That made me proud. Proud that she was proud and that she'd lived to see that, even if her son hadn't. Six years had gone by since I'd stood outside his house that summer night. I was grateful for that moment when she passed away six months later at the age of eighty-eight. But it also brought privilege into sharp focus. My grandparents on my mum's side came from a middle-class upbringing – they knew the world that a good university experience could open up, and they used that knowledge to guide me towards Trinity. For Nanny Haskins, Trinity was inconceivable. I feel lucky to have had both of those contrasting perspectives. I wouldn't have gone to Trinity without the first, and I might have taken it for granted were it not for the second.

Dylan Haskins (TCD 2008–12; History of Art and Architecture and Classical Civilization) is a Peabody and Webby Award-winning BBC commissioner for podcasts such as 'Have You Heard George's Podcast?', 'Where is George Gibney?' and 'I'm Not a Monster' from **Panorama** and **Frontline** (PBS). Before joining the BBC, he worked freelance as a producer and presenter with RTÉ, **The Guardian** and **Other Voices**, and co-hosted the podcast 'Soundings' with Lisa Hannigan. He is a trustee of the Rich Mix east London arts centre and the Borris Festival of Writing and Ideas in Co. Carlow.

Dylan Haskins with his grandmother Elizabeth Haskins at his graduation from Trinity, 2012.

QUANTUM McMUFFIN

ON LEARNING TO LEARN

hal hodson

ON WEEKDAYS in the spring of 2010, I bought breakfast from the McDonald's at the bottom of Grafton Street. I'd arrive by bicycle at 5.30 am. Sometimes, stragglers from the previous night's parties were trailing out clutching bags of chips, their adrenaline ebbing. I always bought the same thing. A Double Sausage and Egg McMuffin consisted then, as it does now, of two pork patties and a puck of egg melted between two halves of an English muffin glued together with a slice of EZ cheese. It came with an OK cup of coffee and a hash brown, the most delightful and dangerous item on the McDonald's menu. I'd wrap the top of the brown paper bag that contained the food around my handlebars, grip it in place while mounting the bicycle and pedal into college.

I don't remember how I came to embrace central Dublin's premium pre-dawn breakfast, but I do remember why. The streets are beautiful before sunlight and traffic take over. You can pedal your bike with no hands, tracing long arcs along damp, empty roads, cutting through pools of halogen lamp-light. Taxis loomed out of the darkness with 'For Hire' signs that glared like a cyclops' eye. Being alone and alert in Dublin as night gave way to morning gave me a feeling of control over time, over the city and over myself.

I needed that. I was in my final year at Trinity, studying astrophysics. I had nearly failed the previous year thanks to a potent mix of arrogance and incompetence. It turned out that while I was OK at thinking about science, I wasn't very good at doing it. My abilities had been tested for the first time that year in the practical project that made up half of the mark. I was useless. My poor supervisor would suggest I go away and do a basic chunk of scientific measurement using the fairly straightforward strategy he laid out. I would come back with what amounted to a science fiction story about the binary star system we were studying. 'Maybe they are spiralling into each other,' I would posit. He would roll his eyes.

I was running before I could walk. My supervisor, a professor of astrophysics called Brian Espey, was telling me what to do and how to do it, and I didn't respect him or the institution we were both part of enough to even recognize my lack of respect. I got an effective zero on the practical segment of the year, dragging my whole grade into the dirt.

Now the potential implications were drawing in on me – bad job, no job, shame. I responded by entering academic crisis mode. Extracurricular activities ended. I stopped tutoring Aoife, the secondary student I had helped with maths and physics for years for extra cash, and apologized to her mother. I stepped away from my beloved Trinity American Football team, which I'd helped grow from nothing over the previous three years. My life fell into a basic rhythm: early mornings, McMuffins and quantum mechanics.

My then-girlfriend was understanding in the face of my newly manic routine. I would leap out of bed at 5 am, fold myself into a grey wool overcoat that I had found at the army surplus, pull on a pair of purple plimsolls that were falling apart and start cycling north through Rathmines. The coat was cut for a man a foot shorter than me but with a bigger chest, and it billowed out behind me like a cape while I pedalled fast towards Dublin's city centre. I worried that its tails were going to get stuck in the back wheel. As the eccentric became quotidian, that bike ride started to create space for the physics problems I was studying to fill my head, my spinning legs pumping equations into my brain.

I worked on those equations in Trinity's only twenty-four-hour study room. It was glassed off from, but still connected to, the main humanities library, perched on a concrete platform that hovered beside the cricket pitch. You could swipe in with your student card any time. I usually arrived at about a quarter to six. The handful of all-nighters were asleep, cheeks gummed to their open textbooks with drool. For a while this one guy was there every morning with headphones on, eyes open, pen scribbling. We never spoke. The presence, and potential observation, of another did not sit well with my embarrassing breakfast habit. He didn't last long, though, and with his departure my sense of control over the universe deepened.

Sometimes the work that followed was a delight. Mornings would evaporate as I crunched through problems about the positions of electrons and laser beams. Electrons are weird. They do not behave like the tangible objects humans interact with every day, or at least they don't if you want to solve undergraduate physics problems about them. Instead of moving through the world smoothly and continuously, like a ball rolling along the ground, electrons jerk from one state to the next, in and out of position. Their behaviour is quantized, discrete, and it moves in steps rather than lines. Their position in the atoms that they comprise is determined by the energetic kicks they get from the outside world. But those positions are discrete and specific. There is no in-between.

Calculations about a single electron can be done with pencil and paper. It must be in a box, or in a vacuum, or the math reaches god-level. Calculating what electrons are doing in the fabric of the real world is effectively impossible. One of the promises of quantum computers, a technology that is only now slipping out of science fiction and into Google Labs, is that they will be able to do these sorts of calculations, making predictions about the fabric of the real world. Predicting the behaviour of people, however, will remain out of reach for some time.

All I had back then was the pencil and paper. The maths would start flowing as my coffee cooled, and the spurs of my early morning softened. I would solve one problem after another correctly. When I got one wrong, I'd be able to trace the root of the mistake, gaining a deeper understanding of the reality that the maths described. On a good day, the afternoon would arrive in a rush of surprise. I'd look up at the clock and see it was 4 pm, rubbing my eyes and looking around at the now-full room. The reality of the last nine hours would wash over me like the plot twist in a film.

Inducing myself into this flow state has been a part of my professional life ever since. The first seeds were sown as I crammed for school exams as a teenager, but Dublin was where I learned to do it for myself, without the attention of parents or teachers. The McDonald's, the hipster greatcoat and the 5 am start were psychological catalysts, bumping my mind into the right state.

My techniques have evolved in the decade since I left Trinity, but some of the themes remain. I still contort my schedule into silly shapes as part of my journalistic writing. Late nights provide the same time dilation as early mornings, even if they feel less healthy to me. Both early mornings and late nights satisfy the stoic in me, pushing through the conventional boundaries of a comfortable life to find that, actually, you can handle it out there. I am writing this part of the essay sitting in *The Economist*'s Hong Kong office at nine minutes past midnight on a Saturday, two cups of coffee in, entirely alone, finally finding focus, a path to concentration through the extreme.

The early-morning routine had made my mind understandable to me, and thereby controllable. But like the toy problem of an electron in a box, those answers applied to a slice of time and space that was so thin it was scarcely real. Flow state was fun, but it did not always work. Much less enjoyable, more painful, was when the morning's passage made itself known, grating against my failure to understand the work. In response, my attention would drag itself away on loop – to the brightening cricket pitch, new arrivals or the entire internet that sat just a click away from me on my laptop. Instead of an enjoyable morning churning through interesting problems, it would be a day without progress. Me at my desk in the back corner, head in hands, books open; students flowing in around me; another coffee break; Trinity's main gates opening to the buses thundering past on College Green, packed with commuters going to work; me, alone and stupid, stuck in my place in the living lattice of Dublin. To keep making progress through that lattice, like an electron, I needed a kick.

That kick came from Trinity. The new knowledge that my morning flow states had brought helped me start to see the college, and in particular its physics institutions, in a new light. I realized, for instance, that CRANN – the Centre for Research on Adaptive Nanostructures and Nanodevices – was at the cutting edge of the science that makes computers run as a seamless part of our lives (trying to understand how the geopolitical and economic interacts with the nanoscopic is basically my job now). I started to understand and respect the scaffolding that had been sitting around me the whole time, just waiting for me to lean into it. I looked up one of Professor Espey's papers. It had been cited by hundreds of other astrophysicists: *The Type Ic Supernova 1994I in M51: detection of helium and spectral evolution*. Supernovae, the phenomena of exploding stars. I had been ignoring people who could explain how and why things like that happened.

I started to go and meet my lecturers, asking them things I didn't understand. Those meetings were some of the most intellectually fulfilling moments of my life. It turns out that the spark of understanding jumping from one person to another is a lot deeper and more magical than cruising through physics problems you already get, no matter how early you woke up to force yourself to do it. Sometimes those sparks could jump through the pages of textbooks, but when that didn't work, I needed people.

With my attention focused on work, I made friends with my course-mates in a way that I had not in my previous three years. I started being able to help some people with physics problems, the process of supporting our small group feeding back into a deepening and improvement of my own understanding of the problems. My old friends I kept, though I saw them less regularly, and for less extended periods of time. The meandering afternoons spent in each other's company were less and less. I drank less.

It turns out that knowledge does not grow continuously, like a walker climbing a hill. Rather, knowledge is absent, absent, absent, until suddenly it snaps into place. Sometimes, that snap came in full flow – a realization delivered to me from my subconscious, processed, I liked to think, while I pedalled to McDonald's that morning. But other times it came as a spark of understanding transmitted between two people, between my lecturers and me, my classmates and me. Sometimes it was encoded in a look, or a gesture, or the tone of voice in the way a lecturer or a classmate said something to me – a wide smile as I asked, 'Is it like this?'

Hal Hodson (TCD 2006–10; Physics with Astrophysics) is **The Economist**'s Asia technology correspondent, focusing on the electronics manufacturing industry and the implications of tensions between America and China. He works on stories about the technologies that shape our lives, the systems that control them and the people who find themselves in the yoke. He joined the paper in 2016 as science and technology correspondent, and before that he worked at **New Scientist** in Boston and London.

CHAMPAGNE AT THE HAIRDRESSERS

alice ryan

IN MY first year studying Business and French at Trinity, the heating stopped working in the Arts Block. Lectures were cancelled and mass migration to the Pav began. The evacuation was mid-stream when our Economics lecturer strode down the wide steps of the lecture hall in a camel coat.

Economics, she proclaimed, assumes that human beings are always capable of making rational decisions. We froze in our tracks (and in our cold toes). Well, she asked, didn't we have coats? We were to put them on, sit down and listen.

Pulling on our hats and scarves, we learned that economics was all about making choices. We had chosen toast over cereal that morning. We had taken the bus over the LUAS. We had ordered tea over coffee. For every choice we'd already made that day, economic theory presumed we'd based our decisions on rationality – that we had weighed up our options and made the choice that maximized our value.

We watched her striding around the room, prodding sleeping Canterbury tracksuits back to life, and knew – even then, in a freezing lecture hall – that rationality was far from what we were witnessing in the real world.

When we started college in 2005, the rationality of national decision-making was at an all-time low. The banks who gave 100 per cent mortgages weren't rational, the government who neglected the basics of bank regulation weren't rational and the 200 students sitting in the Ed Burke lecture theatre about to embark on business degrees were far from rational.

We'd grown up on irrationality. Even if you weren't part of it (which most of us weren't), the prevailing culture encouraged irrational economic behaviour: pensions were a waste of money; everyone should buy-to-rent; you were mad if you didn't pour your life savings into investment apartments in Bulgaria. There was talk of cars for Christmas and blank cheques for eighteenth birthdays. There was a rumour that Girls Aloud had been flown in from London to perform at the twenty-first birthday party of a girl in UCD. But UCD may as well have been Yemen to us. We had our own economic system, and it barely passed Grafton Street. (It stretched to Suffolk Street if you were meeting your mum for tea in Avoca.)

When analysed carefully, it became clear that individuals in the micro-economy of the Arts Block cared primarily and deeply about lunch. Where they were going for lunch, what they were having for lunch and, crucially, who else was going for lunch. And if lunch was the short-term focus, then the Trinity Ball was the long-term concern. Securing your ticket, getting the right dress, ensuring your hair was straightened to within an inch of its existence. We had deep and compelling issues, so it was no wonder that the warnings were slow to sink in.

Even when various lecturers broke it to us that a crash was coming, it was still hard to believe. We knew that economic crises were grim; we'd read John Steinbeck. And in our Leaving Cert history book there was a photo of a wheelbarrow of cash being pushed around the Weimar Republic to pay for a stamp. But these were visible manifestations of economic crises – at that time, people in Ireland were still drinking champagne at the hairdressers – so it was hard to believe that a recession was coming and there'd be no jobs.

Because if there was one thing we knew, it was that we could get a job. It was so easy to get work back then – you could walk up Grafton Street in the morning and start a shift that afternoon. And because the economy was booming there was plenty of the Holy Grail of work: flexible, well-paid jobs that fitted around our busy social lives. We got promotional work handing out Coke cans on Grafton Street, packets of Cadbury buttons in shopping centres and bottles of sugary cider in pubs. We sold ice-cream in Croke Park and pulled pints at festivals all over the country.

Jobs weren't just flexible and well-paid, for the most part they were great fun too. In 2006, a gang of us Trinity students got work as catering staff at the Ryder Cup. We took a bus every morning at 5 am from O'Connell Street to the K Club and arrived home late, still high from all we had seen.

In the plush tee-side suites, we witnessed opulence and behaviour most of us never knew existed. The marquees where banks wined and dined their clients were ten times bigger than most people's dingy flats, and the people in them were bent on good times. One morning, all hell broke loose when a bank executive's wife was told there were no biscuits available, only freshly baked pastries. Earlier that morning I had spotted a commis chef with a tin of USA biscuits at the eighteenth tee. In my shirt and tie, I ran through the crowds to negotiate with him, returning triumphant with a handful of chocolate bourbons. The executive's wife didn't smile or say thank you, but her deeply palpable distress subsided.

On other days, celebrities passed through the fancy marquees. A barman in the know told us to take note of the polite seventeen-year-old we served breakfast to. Six years later, we saw Rory McIlroy again, this time on TV winning the US Open.

On the last night of the Ryder Cup, a group of red-faced, pink-shirt-wearing executives didn't want the party to end. We were exhausted after the long week, and our smiles were wilting. Sensing a revolt, the red faces began to tip us after every drink. By the time we ran for the last bus, we had to stop them from stuffing €100 notes into our hands. They had bought us bottles of champagne, offered us commemorative ties, books and gift bags to keep serving them. Still in our uniforms, we went straight to Temple Bar, danced all night, and splurged our tips on kebabs from Zaytoon – it was the high life. Safe to say that when we started college in 2005, we thought jobs grew on trees. You only had to wake up to get one. But towards the end of that decade, things had started to change.

One day in 2008, I was walking up Grafton Street on my way home from college. Most likely I was deep in thought about what I'd had for lunch or where I would go for lunch tomorrow. There was a queue of people snaking from the newsagent beside St Stephen's Green around the corner and down Grafton Street. Unlike a queue for concert tickets or a book-signing, there was nothing obviously linking this group. Young, old, male, female, Irish and foreign accents made up the human snake. The only thing they had in common was the A4 CV they all held in their hands.

I saw them later on the nine o'clock news. There were people with Masters degrees, one guy had a PhD in Engineering. They were all desperate to get a part-time job in a newsagent. It wasn't a John Steinbeck novel or a wheelbarrow of cash – it was one very long queue of overqualified professionals that flipped the switch in the end. It all started to fall apart from there. Everything our lecturers had been warning us about – our parents' jobs, pensions, investments, our own cushy part-time positions – everything started to crumble. And in the Business department at Trinity, we had front-row seats.

That year – 2008 – we had been assigned a project exploring Ireland's International Financial Services Centre. Each group had to pick a global business that was located in the IFSC. We were to undertake a detailed case study to try to understand why that company had chosen Ireland and the factors that helped them prosper here. My group chose the global investment bank Bear Sterns, who in 2007 employed over 120 people in Dublin between two affiliates: Bear Stearns Bank and Bear Stearns Dublin Development Centre. However, by the time we tried to contact the company to arrange an interview, the address listed on the website was a PO box and the company only had twenty-three employees left in Dublin.

This was the backdrop to which one student (myself) wrote a dramatic article in the *Trinity Times* entitled 'Nothing To Lose but Our Chains?', wondering whether capitalism was in its death throes. A copy of the paper from November 2008 which recently turned up (strategically hidden by myself), mentions everyone from Hugo Chavez to Kim Jong Il. In between slamming George Bush and wondering if Marx was right, I wrote that 'In a year that has seen world markets crash and widespread government intervention in national economies, the question must be asked: are we witnessing the fall of the free market economy?' Spoiler alert: the author concludes that we weren't. But still, she felt the need to ask.

Whether by design or whether it had always been planned, that same year we began studying the Great Depression. We learnt about the wild stock market speculation of the 1920s, banking panics, the gold standard and the inaction of the Federal Reserve. We learnt how FDR had stimulated the US economy by enacting the New Deal. We liked the sound of it. We decided we'd take one of those. We looked forward to the Irish government whipping out their wallet to build all those gleaming new roads, state-of-the-art schools, smart hospitals, glass airports and steel bridges.

Counter-cyclical spending, our professor called it. When an economy was booming, governments reigned in spending and increased taxes. When an economy was in trouble, governments injected the money they had saved during the boom into the economy to stimulate it. It made sense. And boy were we glad to hear that there was a plan to quell the rising tide of uncertainty that was enveloping our friends and family.

There are only three specific lectures that stick in my mind from my time in Trinity. The first, I have already mentioned – sitting in the freezing lecture hall wondering about the mysterious concept of rationality. The second was Michael O'Leary giving a guest lecture in Transport Economics and offering a prize for the most outrageous question. A guy in the back won a €50 flight voucher for asking O'Leary when he had last had a wank. Thankfully, O'Leary declined to answer.

The final lecture I remember was when we were told we weren't going to get any steel bridges. No airports. No schools. No public-works scheme because there was no public money left. It had all been spent during the boom. Our lecturer quoted Charlie McCreevy, Minister for Finance from 1997 to 2004, who had reportedly said, 'If I have it, I spend it.' There was silence in the lecture hall. The class was finished, but we couldn't move and remained glued to our seats. How was it possible that a group of lunch-obsessed economic novices such as ourselves knew about counter-cyclical spending but the people in charge didn't? It was like one of those horror movies where the parents all disappear, and you realize the call is coming from inside the house. We were left in disbelief. There was no back-up plan.

Without the gleaming new roads and steel bridges, for most of us, leaving college at the height of the recession meant leaving the country. According to the Nevin Economic Research Institute, nearly half a million people left Ireland in the six years after April 2008.

Thanks to *Reeling in the Years*, we knew all about emigration; it was when people in bomber jackets with perms queued outside the American embassy for visas. Worse than dodgy haircuts, we knew from Junior Cert history that emigration also meant boats riddled with cholera, typhus and dysentery. Even if you survived that, then you'd be in for slave labour, discrimination and dire poverty. With round-the-clock Skype and cheap flights home, even if we did have to leave, we knew we had it good.

Intrigued by the crash I didn't see coming, I went to London to study Economic History at the LSE and then later worked at the BBC. Most of my contemporaries also moved to London, with some going farther afield to New York, Sydney or Vancouver. As with all economic crashes, economic centres bounced back fastest, and there still seemed to be enough jobs to go around in London. Friends rose up the ranks in accounting and consulting firms, they ran advertising and marketing campaigns and built up social media bases for multinationals.

As the harsh limelight of 2008 faded, the good times in finance seemed to roll around pretty fast again. By 2010, friends who worked as traders in Canary Wharf told of setting their alarms for fifteen-minute naps in the bathroom stalls at work to recover from all-expenses-paid nights out. I remember wondering if we'd somehow imagined it all: the lack of jobs, the need to emigrate, the people carrying boxes out of Lehman Brothers on the news, the long queue of overqualified professionals snaking down Grafton Street desperate for that part-time job in the newsagent. This was compounded by the fact that by the time we'd found our feet abroad, it seemed that even Ireland was almost on the rise again. A few years after I'd left Dublin, I asked a friend who studied at Trinity after me where she'd be going when she graduated – the answer was nowhere. It was strange to think that our fates had been so strongly influenced by graduating during that specific period. For some the die had been cast – they met wonderful partners, got married, had beautiful children with sweet accents and struggle to imagine returning to Ireland. Others, like myself, eventually did come home.

You can spot us returnees a mile away. We sing the praises of our host countries loudly and annoyingly for the first few months and vow to keep up the habits and routines we acquired there. Those returnees from London track and rate coffee shops, obsessing over quality, service and opening hours. They text each other café recommendations like they are giving each other a kidney. Those back from Sydney rent flats in Dún Laoghaire or Howth because they plan to continue surfing/sailing/swimming/kayaking/water skiing after work. By mid-November – when it is pitch black by 3.30 pm, there are squalls in the Irish Sea and the coastguard has to rescue them from near-death – they finally concede to wait for the summer to re-start paddle boarding. The recently returned eventually pipe down about coffee and water sports and row in with the rest of the country to complain about astronomical rent levels and non-existent childcare instead.

Despite the economic prospects of London or the balmy climate of Sydney, Dublin has one up on all these cities. Here, we can walk the cobblestones of Trinity again – even just as visitors. Trinity is a physical reminder of Friday afternoons sitting in the Ussher Library, watching the slow shift of people from the desks beside you to the Pav. Walking under Front Arch brings back memories of Trinity Balls when the college grounds were transformed into a dark and exciting maze while we hid cans of cider beneath tuxes and ballgowns for disposable-camera photos, most of which now sit in drawers gathering dust. All of this took place in a haze of giddy nervousness as we tried to find out who we were and, more importantly, who we wanted to be.

Not long after I came back to Ireland, I found myself wandering down Grafton Street coaxing a precious newborn to sleep. I wheeled my sleeping bundle through Front Arch at some ungodly hour and found myself enveloped in an unexpected but very welcome blanket of familiarity and safety. The towering Campanile, the slipway onto New Square, the statue of Lecky sitting in an oversized chair, his head resting on his giant hand and, in every corner, memories of the person I'd been then. London's economy may bounce back fast, and you may be able to water ski all year round in Sydney, but only Dublin holds the cherished memories of who we were and the possibility of who we can still become.

Trinity BESS ball, 2006. From left: Claire Ryan, Alice Ryan, Cathal Hardiman, Jenny Quinn and James Eagan.

Alice Ryan (TCD 2005–9; Business and French) lives in Dublin with her husband and daughter. After graduating from Trinity, she moved to London where she worked in book publishing and at the BBC. She currently works for The Arts Council of Ireland.